THE POTATO MAN

SOPHIA MARCUS

5-11-08

REVIEW AND HERALD PUBLISHING ASSOCIATION

Washington, DC 20039-0555
Hagerstown, MD 21740

To all who are saints of God

and

To all who are trying to be

and

To all who would like to be

and

To all who are afraid to be

This little story is humbly dedicated.

Copyright © 1986 by
Review and Herald Publishing Association

This book was
Edited by Gerald Wheeler
Designed by Richard Steadham
Cover art by Denny Bond
Type set: 11/12 Melior

PRINTED IN U.S.A.

Library of Congress Cataloging in Publication Data

Marcus, Sophia, 1930-
   The Potato Man.

   1. Shemaiah. 2. Converts, Seventh-day Adventist—
Biography. I. Title.
BX6189.S54M37   1985   248.2′4   85-18442
ISBN 0-8280-0309-2

THE POTATO MAN

Sunday afternoon a man, dressed in his best clothes, slipped around the corner of my house where I was cutting a few pink roses. Setting down a large basket of newly dug potatoes, he grasped my hand in both of his and gave me a warm Eastern greeting.

"How are you, sister? [That's what people in that country called me as a nurse.] You have been gone so long! How are you? How are your parents? Where is Teresa? [Teresa was a friend who lived with me.] How was your work that took you from the hospital these many months?"

His questions came much too rapidly in a language of which I understood but little. Nodding and smiling, I tried to answer him, but had to let him fill in entire lines.

As profusely as my tongue could perform, I thanked him for his kindness in coming, and for the twenty-five pounds of potatoes. Potatoes at times were almost as difficult to find in the markets as were apples on evergreen trees. This was one of those times. Thoughts of baked potatoes, mashed potatoes, potato soup, and potato salad flooded through my mind. What a treat!

When I asked him about his wife and children, he replied, "They are all fine. They send their greeting to you also." He communicated this to me with a big smile and many words that I did not understand. Then he shook my hand again, bowed, and turned to leave by way of the stony road that led out through the swinging gate and past a row of tall gray-green trees.

Taking the basket into the kitchen, I set it on the floor in front of Teresa. "Look at them!" I spoke with delight. "Look what Priest Shemaiah brought us!" She was as excited as I was, also realizing the value of potatoes in that land.

"Let's call him the *Potato Man*," she said with a grin. "That's an honorable name for so generous a gentleman."

A few days later her parents, the Brownings, arrived. It was one of their stops on a world tour. In two weeks Teresa would be leaving with them.

"Where did you get such large, beautiful potatoes?" Mrs. Browning asked.

"Oh, we have a friend who grows them. We call him the Potato Man," her daughter replied, laughing. "He and his family are really nice folks."

That evening he came by with more potatoes. I invited him into the living room and called the Brownings. Around a crackling fire in the fireplace we chatted as best we could. At last he stood and shook hands with each of us, bowed, and went out into the darkness.

"Seems like an interesting person," Mr. Browning said with a twinkle in his eye.

"I surely like his potatoes," I replied.

Some nights later he returned. Again we chatted as awkwardly as a three-legged cow walks. And again he left.

"Why does he come?" Mr. Browning asked.

"That's what *we* want to know," I said. "It's a mystery, really, but I guess he's just being friendly."

Saturday night we heard the same familiar knock. When I opened the door, there stood the Potato Man with a translator. We popped some corn and settled down for a long visit around the fireplace. What could he want? An hour or so went by as he talked about the grain crops, the rain, the bus service, his relatives. The Brownings and I sat and listened—and wondered.

THE REASON

At last the Potato Man cleared his throat. He paused and gazed a long time into the orange flames, while he lightly fingered his white turban.

"Uh," he began, "sister, I have seen you give out many Bibles in my language. You gave me one last spring. I have been reading it for several months. Now I have many questions. Can you answer them for me?"

"We might answer some of them, but I'm sure we can't answer them all. What are your questions?" I asked.

"Oh, priests and our work. I think we aren't doing what God says," he said, hesitating. "But not tonight. I'll ask questions another time. They really bother me. You know I'm one of the priests in the biggest church in this area. When the high priest dies I will be his successor. People trust me. I am a soul father for hundreds of church members. But as I read, I have many questions. I have asked many, many of the priests, but they don't know the answers. Since you're giving Bibles to churches in this area, maybe

5

God means for you to answer my questions. Sometimes I wonder—am I teaching my people what the Bible says? As a leader I must know what to tell them."

He paused while he stared blankly at the glowing embers. "When can you help me?"

"How about Sunday afternoon? That's a good time, isn't it?" I asked.

A frown spread over his face. "Not really." Shaking his head, he stood up and stirred the hot coals with a poker and tossed in another piece of wood.

"When would you like to come?"

"At night," he answered quickly. "When it's very dark." He sat down again.

"Really? Most folks don't like being out in this area at night."

"It's safer for me. I don't want my friends—or my enemies—to know that I'm coming here to study the Bible. It must be in secret."

"So when would you like to come?" I asked.

"Saturday night at seven-thirty. It's very dark then."

"That's a good time. Let's plan that way. Bring your Bible and your questions, and we'll see what we can do. In the meantime, let's ask God to help us all to understand more. There's much I need to learn too. Is this the translator you want?" I inquired.

"Yes, I think he can help us very well."

The two men stood to leave. The Potato Man removed his white turban and then wrapped a peasant's blanket around himself, covering most of his head. Thanking us, they went out into the darkness. The translator walked down the road to the big gate. We watched the Potato Man as he slipped out behind our house and stealthily climbed the barbed-wire fence while a half moon painted bright splotches on dead leaves beneath the shadowy trees.

Back in the living room, Teresa and I picked up the popcorn bowls. "So that's the reason he's coming!" Mrs. Browning commented.

"Took him a while to come around with his request," Teresa added. "This should be rather interesting. I wish I weren't leaving."

"He must have some quite serious questions," her father reflected as he stood warming himself by the dying fire.

That night at family worship we asked God to teach us all. Then we went to bed. As I lay there watching the stars sparkle between the leaves, I wondered—What are his questions? Do I know the answers?

ONE QUESTION

Saturday night we gathered around the fire. When the Potato Man arrived, his translator didn't come, so I asked Brother Thomas, a friend, to help us.

As he leafed through his Bible, our visitor said, "I'm eager for answers."

"Mr. Browning, would you lead us in prayer?" I asked.

Teresa's father prayed that the Spirit of God would

teach us all as we studied, and thanked Him for the Holy Bible, which He gave to us by inspired writers.

"Now we're ready for questions," I said to the priest.

As he nervously fingered the edge of his blanket, he smiled, then said, "Why don't you teach me from the beginning of the Bible?"

"You mean the first chapter of Genesis?"

He nodded.

"Is there anything you especially want to know about Genesis 1?"

"No, let's just read it and talk about it."

So we opened our Bibles, and I suggested that he begin reading.

" 'In the beginning God created the heaven and the earth,' " he intoned. " 'And the earth was without form, and void; and darkness was upon the face of the deep. And the Spirit of God moved upon the face of the waters. And God said, Let there be light: and there was light. And God saw the light, that it was good: and God divided the light from the darkness. And God called the light Day, and the darkness he called Night. And the evening and the morning were the first day' " (Genesis 1:1-5).

He stopped. "Do you believe this?" he asked.

"Yes!" we all chorused.

"So do I," he said, and continued to the second, third, and fourth days.

"Do you believe this?" he then questioned.

We all nodded.

"So do I," he said, and read on about the creation of fish and fowls, mammals, and finally man and woman.

"We have a wonderful God, don't we?" Mr.

Browning commented. "He has tremendous power and great concern."

The priest nodded, his face radiating joy. Then it clouded. "Let's go on to chapter 2," he urged. "That's the seventh day. It says God rested on the Sabbath, the seventh day. Are there two Sabbaths every week, or is there just one?"

"What leads you to believe that there are two?" I asked.

"We priests teach the people that there are two Sabbaths—Saturday and Sunday. Remember I talked to you last spring one day? You told me you'd give me $10 if I could find any place in the Bible that says we should have two Sabbaths each week. I've looked and looked, but I can't find anything like that. Why am I teaching this to my people?"

I shook my head. "I don't know. Why are you?"

He stared into the fire. "Tradition says we should. The saints say we should. Our patriarch says we should," he said slowly. Then he began telling stories found in tradition. A half hour went by. Then an hour. Once in a while he would pause questioningly and remark, "That's what tradition says."

Mr. Browning would interject kindly, "But what about the Bible, God's own Word? What does it say?"

"But tradition says . . ." Our friend kept coming back to it until the fire had burned to little more than embers.

After a brief closing prayer, the priest removed his turban, wrapped himself in his blanket, and vanished into the darkness. Brother Thomas, his translator, headed down by himself to the big gate.

ANCIENT LIBRARY

A week went by. Another Saturday night. Another knock. There stood the Potato Man and Brother Thomas.

Again we all gathered around the fire. After a prayer asking God to teach us, the priest said, "Let's talk about Adam and Eve, the story in Genesis 2 and 3."

We opened our Bibles and read a verse or two.

Then our friend responded, "Tradition says . . . " I marveled at how much he knew about the tradition of his faith. A half hour or so went by.

"You have learned a great deal about tradition," I commented. "Where did you learn so much?"

"We have many holy books that tell us these things," he explained. "Do you remember those sacred volumes we priests showed you up in our little library by our church?"

As I nodded I remembered that the priests had told us that we should come before 6:00 A.M., and that we must not eat or drink anything from sundown the evening before. We had arrived at sunrise. "Have you had anything to eat or drink?" they had asked.

After assuring them that we had not, they had led us to the special room where they stored dozens of ancient books, handwritten on parchment and beautifully illustrated with hand-painted pictures of the saints. Some of the volumes were 500 years old. The ones they felt to be the most sacred were wrapped in exquisite silks, many with gold threads woven into the rich colors.

10

"Do you have a Bible?" I had asked.

"No, we haven't," they had answered, "but we have the four Gospels—Matthew, Mark, Luke, and John." Quickly they brought me four books, each larger than any unabridged dictionary I've seen. Church scribes had carefully traced each letter onto the parchment by means of shaped bamboo sticks and homemade ink. The books contained pages and pages of flawless, beautiful writing. Artists had painted colorful, full-page illustrations here and there throughout the four volumes.

I had noted that the priests handled the Gospels carefully and reverently, yet not as much so as when they touched the books about tradition and the saints.

"You don't wrap these in beautiful cloth?" I had asked as I fingered the gaudy cotton fabric that covered them.

"No," they had answered seriously. "These are not as sacred or precious as the books of saints and miracles and tradition."

I had given them several copies of the entire Bible as a gift when I had left.

Yes, I knew what Priest Shemaiah,* the Potato Man, referred to when he asked, "Do you remember those sacred books we showed you?"

Then he continued with more tradition. Although occasionally one of us would interrupt, "But the Bible says . . . ," he would go on telling about his people's heritage.

Nine o'clock came. "I guess we should quit this and go home." With a smile he stood.

---

* It is the custom among Priest Shemaiah's people to carefully use a title before the name to show honor and respect. I have followed this practice in this book.

We prayed, then followed the two men to the door. "May I come next Saturday night?" the priest whispered as he stepped out into the blackness.

"Yes," we whispered back, and the two were gone.

"What were his questions?" Teresa asked when we were again in the living room.

"That's what I want to know," I replied.

EARLY SERVICE

After the two men left, the Brownings and I stood around the fireplace. "Seems like a friendly person," Mr. Browning commented. "I wonder what he wants to know."

"I'm going to bed," I said, changing the subject. "I want to go visit his church tomorrow morning. You folks are all leaving on Monday. Do you want to come with me early tomorrow?"

"I do," Teresa said. "One last time! I've been there many times, but I'll probably never get there again."

"Well, I'll go too," Mr. Browning added. "I've visited several churches in this area, but I'd like to see one more."

"I'm sleeping in," his wife announced with a yawn.

"Five o'clock comes early. Let's go to bed!" I remarked, starting down the hall.

Early the next morning while the stars still

studded the sky we awakened. Off in the distance we heard a rooster's faint crow. A donkey brayed nearer by. Birds twittered their early-morning greetings. From nearly a mile away floated the chants of priests as drums and tambourines beat time for their clapping and their ancient religious dances. It was time to be on our way. Jackets on, we hurried along our rocky path out to the dusty road that bordered a dewy pasture. Peasants, staffs in hand, blankets over their shoulders, silently sped along, alone or in little groups. We turned off the dusty road to climb the steep hillside. Now sharp stones covered the road as it wound its way along low rock walls where delicate pink jewelweed blossoms, wet with dew, were beginning to lift their heads in the early-morning light. Songbirds called to one another in the bushes not far away. Up and up we went. The beautiful low, slow beat of the drums grew louder now. Occasionally we heard loud, rhythmic clapping, with the sudden joyful shout of praise as the singers came to a crescendo on one of the psalms of David. There was a beauty in it that I loved. Nowhere else had I seen this kind of praise service—dignified, almost majestic—that had its roots in the Jewish worship of Old Testament times.

At last we stood on top of the hill. The bright-orange sun rose in full view above the hills beyond. Quietly we walked up the stone steps where a priest greeted us. Taking our shoes off, we went in stocking feet into the nave of the church. The members kissed the doorsills after making the sign of the cross. Then they prostrated themselves on the floor at the door. After a moment they would stand. A priest would hold out a brass cross to them and they would kiss it.

Entering the church, they would kiss the walls here and there. That done, they would bow before a large picture of the virgin Mary.

Only the devout, "holy" members were allowed inside the church. Few women were there, and most of them were nuns. They stood in one part of the nave that was separated, by a wall perhaps five feet high, from what was called the Holy Place.

Beyond the Holy Place was the Most Holy Place, where only the officiating priests could enter. The choir of priests stood in another part of the nave adjoining the Holy Place.

The men not in the choir stood in the Holy Place during the worship service. For some reason they always invited Teresa and me to come inside the Holy Place, where they provided us with chairs.

And so, as usual, we went into the nave, put our shoes in a special place, then slipped quietly into the Holy Place, where our friend the Potato Man brought chairs for the three of us. He greeted us warmly, then joined the choir as they sang psalms. We sat, and stood at times, reading our Bibles while they read their prayer books in low tones.

When the service began, a priest dressed in colorful robes stood in front reading from a parchment Gospel of John in the ancient language used for all religious worship. Almost no one could understand it. The reading finished, a student-priest carried the closed Gospel around, and each person kissed it. He knew that we regarded the Book as holy but not as an object of worship, so he quietly passed us by.

Then came the liturgical prayers. Standing, the people recited the Lord's Prayer in the same ancient language. Then they prostrated themselves before the

14

painting of the virgin Mary. A number of times they stood and bowed. We had learned that when they stood, they were worshiping God, while when they bowed, they were worshiping Mary. So we stood when they did and sat when they bowed. They seemed to understand that we were a little different but that we too were Christians and loved God very much.

Since I had to be on duty at the hospital at seven-thirty Sunday mornings, we left a little before seven. By this time hundreds of women waited outside the church on one side, and hundreds of men on the other.

As we worked our way back down the hill, people smiled and greeted us warmly as they hurriedly passed us on their way to church. We had grown to anticipate Sunday mornings, when we could climb the mountain and worship God with the people that we loved. Many of them had been our patients. It was good to see that they were able to be up and walking again.

The next day the Brownings left. The Potato Man had stopped briefly Sunday afternoon to tell them Goodbye. Although we missed Teresa, life would have to continue without her.

LEARNING TRADITION

The following Saturday night we once more gathered by the fireside. The priest and Brother Thomas sat on the sofa. I took my favorite place on an orange hassock and leaned against the warm bricks of the fireplace. Martha, who now lived with me since Teresa had gone, was busy in the kitchen.

Priest Shemaiah fingered his Bible as he remarked, "You like coming to our church, don't you?"

"Yes," I answered. "You like your church too, don't you?"

"Oh, I do! The high priest reared me from childhood, so I've always gone to the big church on the hill. He is very pleased that I have given my life to do God's work. And he has given me many responsibilities in the church."

"What are some of the things you do?" I inquired.

"I am in charge of seeing that everything goes well for the choir, though I'm not the leader. I see that things are in order for the service. The high priest depends upon me to keep the priests and choir happy. And, of course, I help with mass. When the high priest is gone, I am the one who changes the bread and wine into the body and blood of Christ." He said this with subdued awe in his voice. "I give the bread to the people and I eat some of the bread and drink the wine. Also I have several hundred people that I am soul father for. It is wonderful to work for God.

"Well, let's study the Bible," he suggested.

16

"All right. Brother Thomas, will you pray?" I asked.

"Our Father, we are thankful for this precious Book that You have given us. We ask You to be with us while we study it. There are many things we don't understand. If we find that we need to change something that we are doing, help us to be willing to do it. We know that You alone forgive sins. Please forgive us for our sins and help us to live as Your children should. We thank You for Jesus, our Saviour. We pray in His name. Amen."

"I want to ask some questions," the priest began. "Sister, why don't you cross yourself before we pray? Why don't you pray to the saints? Why don't you pray to Saint Mary? Why do you always pray in Jesus' name? How can you pray directly to God? You say anything you want to. How is it that you ask *Him* to forgive your sins? We teach our people to come to the priests. Each member has a certain soul father to whom he confesses. I've visited your church a few times long ago. You don't have a picture of Saint Mary there. Anybody you choose in the congregation prays, or the pastor prays. They all ask God to forgive sins. For many years we thought you people were Muslims. But you believe the Gospels and pray in Jesus' name. You're *not* Muslims—are you?" he sighed deeply as the lines of worry changed into a smile.

"No, I am not a Muslim, though I have known many Muslims and respect them very highly," I replied.

"I have asked many priests in my church and the other churches about this. They just shake their heads and say 'We don't know.' Some of them are curious now and are trying hard to find the answers in the

Bibles you gave them. We have spent hours sitting in the sun on the porch steps of the church reading and talking. But we can't find any place where it says to keep two Sabbaths each week or to pray to Saint Mary. We searched for the place that says we priests should forgive sins. I tell you, sister, we can't find anything we look for! Either we are right or we are wrong!" Shaking his head, he groaned, then smiled pleadingly.

I waited.

"Now tradition says . . . " he resumed. Then he began to tell harrowing stories of people who failed to confess to their priests, of those who did not do penance, or those who ignored the church.

Nearly two hours had passed when he stood up and said, "It's time to go." After prayer he left.

"This man is full of tradition," I said to Brother Thomas. "It's interesting to hear, but why does he come? He did ask some questions tonight, but answered them all with tradition."

The man shook his head. "I don't know why he comes. He seems to have questions, but all we do is talk."

"Well, anyway, we have some good times, even if we don't understand it."

Such went the visits for the next four Saturday nights. He was a first-class teacher in tradition. His lessons opened up many new channels of thought. But the thing that made me think long into the night was how far tradition often is from the Bible that he brought each time he visited.

In the meantime I continued to attend his church as often as I could. He wanted to do God's will and so did I. At his church I often prayed that we would all understand God's Word.

"Maybe the problem is the translator," I finally decided. "I'll hunt for a different one before next Saturday night."

VISITING TRANSLATOR

That week a friend of mine traveled through to visit many of his old friends, and stayed with some neighbors. Since he knew both the Potato Man's language and mine, I asked him to translate for us the following night. He agreed. When I told Thomas he could have a night off, the idea pleased him.

Saturday night the priest arrived in the black of darkness with more potatoes. Thanking him, I handed them to Martha, who took them to the kitchen, where she had work to do.

Just then my visiting friend Brother David arrived to translate. After introductions we sat down by the fire.

"Well," the Potato Man said, "let's really study the Bible tonight. I have *many* questions."

"All right," I replied. "Would you like to pray before we begin?"

Shaking his head, he murmured, "I don't know how."

Brother David prayed instead.

"Now for your questions." I turned toward the priest.

"I want to know—" He stopped and rubbed his forehead. "I want to know—" He put his head in his hands in deep thought. "I want to know," he repeated slowly, "why do I ask people to bow down on the floor seventy times when they come and confess to me that they have done something wrong? Why do some priests have them bow three hundred times?"

"I don't know," I replied. "Why do you?"

"What does your Bible say?" Brother David asked.

"My Bible says that—well—what is it? I'll find it."

He leafed back and forth in his Bible until he located the place that he had underlined. "Here it is. I've been reading it for months, but I don't understand it."

"Will you read it to us?" I suggested.

" 'If we confess our sins, he is faithful and just to forgive us our sins, and to cleanse us from all unrighteousness.' That's 1 John 1:9. It doesn't say anything about bowing down or paying money or fasting. And in the Lord's Prayer Jesus taught His disciples to say, 'Forgive us our debts, as we forgive our debtors.' He didn't say 'Forgive us our debts as we bow down seventy times.' Sometimes very old people come. They can hardly get down once. I feel I can't ask them to bow seventy times, so I'll tell them thirty or forty. I watch them and count. It's cruel. I can't find any place in the Bible that says to do this. Why am I doing it?"

However, he didn't pause for an answer but changed the subject and began telling frightening stories from tradition. Occasionally he would chuckle as he would relate his tales.

"But the Bible says—" I would start to say as he would slow before beginning a new illustration.

"This is human tradition. The Bible is God's own revelation to man."

Looking at me pleasantly, he would continue with his topic. Again and again Brother David would repeat, "But what about the Bible?"

The priest talked until nine o'clock. Then he stood to leave.

"Let's pray," I said. "Our Father in heaven, there are so many things we do not understand in the Bible. Help us to learn what You want us to. Teach us the proper use of tradition. We thank You for forgiveness of sin. Forgive us for the wrongs we have done and for neglecting to do what really is Your will. We pray in the name of Jesus. Amen."

"Do you have a flashlight?" the priest asked.

"Yes."

"Could you hold it a few seconds while I climb the fence? I got hung out there last time when I tried to jump down from the tree where the top wires are nailed. We'll do it quickly and hope that no one sees us."

Out into the night we went. "See you next Saturday night," he whispered.

"All right," I replied. The job done, I returned to David, who stood on the front porch.

"That man surely is full of tradition," he remarked. "I don't think he is really interested in the Bible. Maybe he has some other reason for coming."

"Thanks for helping," I called as he started home. "Some other reason for coming—what could it be?" I pondered. "He's already agreed to come next week. I can't say No."

VISITING PATIENT

The next Saturday night brought Brother Thomas and the Potato Man to the front door again. With Priest Shemaiah was another priest whom he introduced as Priest Peter, his brother-in-law. Both took Bibles from under their peasants' blankets as we sat down in the living room.

Our prayer finished, Brother Thomas went to the hallway to answer a knock at the door. An ex-monk greeted him, then explained, "I've come to see the sister. After she treated me at the clinic last week, she told me that she'd like to hear my story." The two men sat down by the fire.

"I just came to visit," the man named John explained as we made introductions.

"Brother John, you used to be a monk, didn't you? Why aren't you one now?" I asked.

"Yes, I used to be, but not anymore."

"Why?"

"Oh, that's too long a story."

The Potato Man, who had his head in his hands, suddenly straightened up. "You were a monk?" he echoed. "Why aren't you now?"

"That's a long story—too long," Brother John repeated.

"No! no!" both the priests chorused. "We'll stay here all night to listen!" the Potato Man pleaded. Martha, who was working at the dining room table, looked up and laughed.

"Why don't you go ahead and tell your story?" I suggested. "Brother Thomas can translate for me."

I wish I could remember everything that the man told us during the next two hours, for it was one of the most exciting accounts I have ever heard.

"I had spent years as a monk in a monastery out on an island in a huge lake," he began. "We had prayer services many times a day and often stayed up all night to pray or to dance and chant sacred music. Also we fasted a great deal, and of course none of us was married. No women were allowed even to touch the island. We wore old clothes and often walked barefoot on sharp rocks. But we were happy to do all this because we thought God required it for our salvation. Though we loved the Gospels, somehow what we did and what we read in them didn't fit. I wondered about it all for years." The man paused, reflecting.

I do not recall how he found a Bible, but he told how he read until he felt convinced that God had a different plan for his life. Eventually he wanted to escape, but the island was carefully guarded, as was the monastery.

"The days and weeks went by," Brother John recalled. "I spent my prayer time asking God to help me to run away. Since I was one of the leaders, I had many responsibilities. One night I was to ring the large bell at midnight to call all the monks to prayer. It was extremely dark as I pulled on the rope. I rang it extra long and hard, for it occurred to me that when all the monks were gathered for prayer, I could escape, for they wouldn't see me back by the bell tower. While I was ringing I was thinking. Then I gave a few extra rings for joy.

"When I stopped I could hear them chanting. I knew they were all inside, for they didn't begin chanting until all were present.

"As fast as I could I ran through the forest and down to the water where there were several small canoes. Quickly I untied one, got into it, and began to paddle. About two hours later I reached the shore. Leaving the boat tied where the monastery always kept its boats when the monks came to buy food, I went up to the town. Since I knew many people there, I decided to flee to the countryside before morning. At last I arrived at a place where I felt I could live safely."

Brother John talked on and on about what he had discovered in the Bible, often so fast that Brother Thomas could scarcely keep up with the translation. He told how he had exchanged religious tradition for the Bible. As he pointed out the differences between the two, the Potato Man pulled his blanket up from behind him and brought it over his head and down to his knees. From under his "tent" he let out a painful wail—"Oh! Oh! Oh!"

As the man spoke of Mary and the saints, more heartrending wails issued from under the blanket. Brother John told of *his* questions and *his* anguish in searching, and then of his joy when he found answers. Occasionally he would laugh at himself when he recalled his dilemma.

The evening wore on with the Potato Man at times out of his "tent," laughing, and at other times under it, mourning. Brother John left almost nothing undiscussed. Fasting. Baptism. Monkhood. Eternally burning hellfire. Praying for the dead. Two Sabbaths. Mass. And Saint Mary. On and on he went, with tears in his eyes one moment, and laughter the next. I shall never forget the cries of the Potato Man at each new subject. Priest Peter simply sat and listened intently, nodding now and then when he agreed.

At nine-thirty I said, "We're all about worn out! It's time for bed. What an interesting story you have to tell, Brother John! I'm so glad you shared it with us. Will you pray with us before you leave, please?"

Then he and Brother Thomas went down the road and the two priests went out to climb the fence while I held the flashlight. The visiting priest, Peter, had said scarcely a word. I hoped he would pour oil on Priest Shemaiah's wounds.

THE DEBATE

Three nights after the ex-monk had related his story, Martha heard a timid knock on our door. When she opened it, there stood the Potato Man. "Come right in," she invited. He stepped in and asked, "Where's the sister?"

Hearing him, I came from the kitchen. "Please, sister," he said, evidence of something troubling him in his face and his voice. "I must talk to Brother John. But I don't dare go to find him or be seen entering his house. Can you have someone call him for me? May we visit in your house?"

"Oh, yes! that's fine," I replied, wondering at the worry all over his usually smiling countenance.

Martha went outside and found a friend who was willing to go get the ex-monk. Soon Brother John appeared. We left him and the priest in the living room, Martha and I returning to the kitchen. We could hear them speaking in low tones. As time went on John's voice became more intense and louder while the priest's had a pleading tone that sounded almost desperate.

About an hour had passed when the two men stood in the doorway to the kitchen.

"Sister, he's impossible! He won't listen to me!" John exclaimed bitterly.

Shemaiah—that kind, generous, serious priest who had brought us so many good potatoes—looked a picture of anger and pain that I had never imagined possible. "I can't reason with him," he choked. "I don't ever ever want to discuss another thing!" He stood staring at his feet.

"But, sister, I can't do a thing for a man who isn't honest enough to get rid of all his tradition at once and follow the pure gospel of Jesus Christ," Brother John explained. "What does this man think he wants me to do for him? I tell you I can't do a thing!" John exclaimed.

Feeling exceedingly sorry for both of them, I laughed and said, "Both of you need to go home and get some sleep. You're too tired to even think. Go home and pray about it. It will all work out later."

Thoroughly beaten, the priest went out the back kitchen door without so much as a nod to Brother John. For a few minutes the former monk lingered. "He's not sincere. He's so ignorant you can't reason with him," the upset man complained. "You're wasting your time, and so am I!"

"Well, I don't know about wasting my time," I replied. "It's nice to have friends, and friends take time. Don't be so hard on him."

Still shaking his head in confusion, Brother John departed. "O God," I prayed that night, "whatever it is that is troubling them, please help them to get it straightened out."

The following Saturday night the priest did not come, nor did he send any message. All evening I waited. Had our friendship ended?

Next morning I arose early. Two friends and I made our way up the hill to the church. There was a strangeness about the place that morning. We heard no drums beating, no chanting or clapping.

Taking our shoes off at the doorway, we entered the nave. Only a dozen or so singers waited in the choir area where usually we had observed seventy-five or a hundred. They seemed uncertain about what to sing and who should do it. I looked around for our friend, who usually got things organized, but he was nowhere in sight. Someone else brought us chairs, and we sat down in the Holy Place as usual. Half an hour later Priest Shemaiah finally arrived. Shaking hands, he whispered that he had not come the night before because he was at a friend's house. "Why not come this evening?" I suggested. He nodded, then went and sat down in a corner. Nervously he pulled at the edges of his blanket as he stared at the floor. He appeared to be quite sick.

"What's the matter with him?" one of my friends whispered.

There seemed to be no order in anything. "He must really carry a lot of responsibility," I said to myself. "It shows when he's unable to function."

Soon thereafter we had to leave. "Strange service today," a person with me commented.

"Yes," I agreed. "What will he say tonight?"

CENSURED

He sat down on the couch beside Brother Thomas that Sunday evening. Resting his chin in his hands—something he seemed always to do when he was deep in thought—he stared at the crackling fire. Then he straightened up and with a tone of sadness said, "The day after Brother John and I were here was Saint Michael's Day. I went up to the church—" During a long pause tears welled up in his eyes. Then he choked out the words, "They put me out of the church. That was Thursday."

"For what?" I exclaimed.

"Well," he replied wearily, "I had read my Bible so much that I lost interest in the rituals of the church service. For weeks I've not been able to generate any enthusiasm. The other priests noticed, and began talking about it. They observed that I asked more and more questions. I love my church and didn't mean to make trouble. I was just trying to discover truth because I want to follow Jesus. I thought they'd want to find truth too. It seemed to me that we could make a few changes and everything in our worship would be the way God says He wants it."

He sighed and continued, "Since it was a holy day, hundreds of people were there. Of course, all of us inside the church were to take Communion. When the high priest offered me the bread, I shook my head and whispered that I was sick—that I had a fly in my mouth. Really, I didn't have, but there is a rule that if a fly gets in one's mouth on the morning of Communion he cannot participate. I thought that would get me out of trouble. The district governor, along with other dignitaries, was there beside me listening to everything. Finally, I took the bread and ate it. Then a fly *did* get in my mouth. It was terrible!"

Priest Shemaiah glanced up with his tear-filled eyes and went on. "The high priest called me to one side and excommunicated me. He didn't say for how long, but told me that I must go to the church court tomorrow. Terrible! Terrible!

"The high priest has brought me up as his own son. I love him! Oh, I love him! And I love my church. What shame! What shame!"

Then he added, "Day before yesterday the high priest's cow died. They say he's being punished for my sins."

"Do they know that you are coming here?" I asked.

"No."

For a long while he sat in deep thought. At last he said, "I don't know what to do. I have to have a church, and I must learn more about the Bible. Can you tell me what is wrong with my church? Brother John told me so much I am sick. Do you have more?"

"My brother," I replied, "let's read what God promises you tonight and tomorrow. Turn to Isaiah 41:13."

He did so and read slowly, " 'For I the Lord thy God will hold thy right hand, saying unto thee, Fear not; I will help thee.'

"That's for me?" he asked with a faint smile.

"Yes, for you. That's like God to promise you help. Let's read Isaiah 43:1, 2. Brother Thomas, please read what God says there."

The translator read: " 'Fear not: for I have redeemed thee, I have called thee by thy name; thou art mine. When thou passest through the waters, I will be with thee; and through the rivers, they shall not overflow thee: when thou walkest through the fire, thou shalt not be burned; neither shall the flame kindle upon thee.' "

"Now I'll read Deuteronomy 33:27," I said. " 'The eternal God is thy refuge, and underneath are the everlasting arms.' God will be with you. He says in Hebrews 13:5 that He will never leave us nor forsake us."

The priest nodded and carefully wrote each reference in a little notebook that he carried. Then standing, he said, "I must be going. It is getting late. Let's pray—you *will* pray for me, won't you?"

We bowed our heads and asked God to show him what to do and what to say.

Then, shaking hands, he cautioned, "Don't bring a flashlight this time. I've found a more secluded place where I can crawl under."

With that, he was gone.

COURT

It was eight-thirty when the priest arrived the following Saturday night. Quickly he explained that the church court the previous Monday had appointed several priests in different areas to spy on him. While he was sure that they didn't know that he was visiting us, he had decided to wait until later when they would probably be quietly at home.

"I want to tell you about the court," he sighed. "One asked me, 'How are you?' I answered, 'The fly is still in my mouth.' Another asked, 'Are you sick?' I said, 'No.' Then one said, 'Where have you been—on a trip, where you learned all this?' I told him, 'No, only to the city.' Then they said, 'What shall we do?' I said, 'Do what you want to do. I only want to follow Jesus.' They answered, 'You act as if you don't care.' I replied that my greatest care is to obey my Saviour.

"They asked me many questions. Then one said, 'Where is your soul father?' I told them that I didn't know. Someone said, 'You should go and find him and confess your sins.' But I asked them why I should confess before a man when only God can forgive sins.

"I read Acts 5:30, 31 to them—I have it marked here in my Bible: ' "The God of our fathers raised up Jesus, whom ye slew and hanged on a tree. Him hath God exalted with his right hand to be a Prince and a Saviour, for to give repentance to Israel, and forgiveness of sins." ' Next I turned to Ephesians 1:7: ' "In whom we have redemption through his blood, the forgiveness of sins, according to the riches of his grace." ' And I read Psalm 130:3, 4: ' "If thou, Lord, shouldest mark iniquities, O Lord, who shall stand? But there is forgiveness with thee, that thou mayest be feared." ' Finally I showed them 1 John 1:9: ' "If we confess our sins, he is faithful and just to forgive us our sins, and to cleanse us from all unrighteousness." '

"When I had finished, they asked me, 'Where are the people that you are soul father for—don't they confess to you?' I replied, 'I am not God; I have no right to ask them to confess to me. I have told them one by one to confess their sins to God, who is in heaven and who is here beside them.'

"The high priest then said, 'We should all pray together for you.' I asked him why. 'We need to ask God to forgive you,' he said. But I answered, 'If there is something for which I must be forgiven, I must ask God for myself. If you want to pray for light that I will find the truth from God, I will be happy to pray for that with you,' I told them. So we all prayed.

"Then someone suggested, 'Let's fast for forty days. We will eat nothing until noon each day and we will eat no meat or animal products. We'll pray for light for you every day for forty days.'

"I told them I'd be happy to join them, but that I would fast in secret, for that is what Jesus said to do. I read to them from Matthew 6:17: ' "But thou, when thou fastest, anoint thine head, and wash thy face; that thou appear not unto men to fast, but unto thy Father which is in secret: and thy Father, which seeth in secret, shall reward thee openly." Only the committee and one or two others will know that I'm fasting, I explained to them.

"They told me that I cannot participate at all in church activities for the next forty days. I may sit in a corner and listen. At the end of that time, they will decide what next to do.

"Last week the provincial patriarch and a church adviser came to visit our church. The adviser called me to one side and told me that I must obey, but the patriarch said to me in secret, 'My son, if you are doing this because you have studied seriously and found new truth, then you should listen to your conscience, and no one should bother you. But if you are doing as Cain did and you are offering God something you hope will please Him, but you don't really care, then a curse will rest upon you. I will be back in two months to hear the reasons for your faith.'

"So that's the story." He smiled and released a long, deep sigh while he wiped the tears from his eyes. "I did nothing wrong, only asked questions to find truth," he reflected quietly.

SHEPHERD AND SHEEP

Crushed, the priest sat fingering his brass cross as he stared blankly at the smoke curling up the chimney. "I love them all; they are my brothers. They just don't understand me." As he tried to comprehend the situation he shook his head.

"Don't you think they *want* to follow Jesus?" I asked quietly.

He nodded.

"Maybe they need to see you awhile, loving and helping them even though they appear to be against you. If they are fasting and praying for you, they must care much about you."

Again he nodded.

"They don't mind your going to church, do they?"

"No, I just can't help."

"Well, even though it's embarrassing, maybe you should continue to go. You can sit in a corner and read your Bible and pray, can't you?"

Our friend straightened up in his chair. "Yes, I

will go. I love them; I love my church; I love God. I will go and worship with them and pray for light. That's what I will do. Now let's read the Bible. You read something."

"Let's turn to John 10, beginning at verse 1," I suggested. We all opened our Bibles. "Brother Thomas, would you read aloud down to verse 16?"

The presence of Jesus seemed near to us as he read the parable of Jesus, the Good Shepherd.

"This is a precious passage for us this evening," I remarked when we had finished. "Jesus says He is the shepherd. His followers are the sheep. He does not say this to demean us as human beings or to lord it over us. David also, by the inspiration of the Holy Spirit, tells us in Psalm 23 what it is like to have the Lord as our shepherd.

"What Jesus is saying in the Gospel of John is that He is the one who cares for us, who keeps us from being lured away or stolen by the evil one. Because the Shepherd does this, His sheep learn to love Him. They come to know His voice, and they follow *Him* and no one else.

"Then beginning in verse 7 He tells us that He is the door to the sheepfold. There is only one door, one way into the fold, and Jesus says that He is that entrance. He is the only way the sheep can find safety from those who would abandon them or who would actually harm or destroy them.

"Beautifully He says in verses 14 and 15, 'I am the good shepherd, and know my sheep, and am known of mine. As the Father knoweth me, even so know I the Father: and I lay down my life for the sheep.' But He goes on to say that some sheep are not yet in the fold, but He, the shepherd, will bring them in.

"Tonight we can know that Jesus cares about us, each one. We will hear His voice as we listen, and we will follow Him if we love Him."

"I have heard His voice," Priest Shemaiah said softly. "I want to follow Him all the way—wherever He leads me."

ABOUT GOD

Early the next morning some friends and I went up to the church to worship. Someone brought us chairs as usual. Our priest friend arrived a little late on purpose to avoid discussion before the service. After greeting us warmly as usual, he then sat down in a corner.

The choir sang somewhat better than the previous Sunday when we had visited, but there were few singers even yet. The priest who read from the Gospel became so confused that another priest came and finished the passage. The altar boy almost dropped the Gospel as he took it around for people to kiss. Such tension filled the air that it was a relief to leave when the service ended. I longed for the peace of days gone by.

Late that evening Priest Shemaiah with his brother-in-law Priest Peter knocked at our door. Brother Thomas had already arrived.

"My brother-in-law has come again to study," the Potato Man explained. "We talked and read for hours in a secluded place, trying to understand the Bible. Tonight we want to know: What is God like?"

After Thomas prayed, asking God to help us comprehend His Word, I began, "We learned a little last time about what God is like when we read from John 10. We found that Jesus, the Good Shepherd, loves His sheep—His people. He protects them. He saves them. He even said He gives His life for His sheep. Remember we mentioned Psalm 23? You both have memorized that."

They nodded. Then Priest Peter remarked, "But that's about Jesus. What about *God*? Isn't He much different from Jesus?"

"The apostle Philip thought Jesus had a different character from that of His Father. Let's turn to John 14:8-10 and see what Jesus told him. Priest Peter, would you read it?"

The brother-in-law found the passage. " 'Philip saith unto him, Lord, shew us the Father, and it sufficeth us. Jesus saith unto him, Have I been so long time with you, and yet hast thou not known me, Philip? he that hath seen me hath seen the Father; and how sayest thou then, Shew us the Father? Believest thou not that I am in the Father, and the Father in me? the words that I speak unto you I speak not of myself: but the Father that dwelleth in me, he doeth the works.' "

"Jesus came to reveal what the Father is like," I explained. "He says clearly, 'He who has seen me has seen the Father.' Now let's turn to John 10. Priest Shemaiah, will you read verses 27-30?"

" 'My sheep hear my voice, and I know them, and they follow me: and I give unto them eternal life; and they shall never perish, neither shall any man pluck them out of my hand. My Father, which gave them to me, is greater than all; and no man is able to pluck them out of my Father's hand. I and my Father are one.' "

"Yes, both the Father and the Son care about the sheep. Let's look at John 3:16. Brother Thomas, would you read it?"

The translator read slowly: " 'For God so loved the world, that he gave his only begotten Son, that whosoever believeth in him should not perish, but have everlasting life.' "

"God loved first, then gave," I commented. "He did not have to do it. What could make Him do such a thing simply to give sinful people a chance to live with Him? He did it because He loved. That's the only explanation. The Father wants us with Him—every bit as much as Jesus does. Turn to James 1:17. It says, 'Every good gift and every perfect gift is from above, and cometh down from the Father of lights.' The Father loves to give us good gifts!"

Shemaiah was busily underlining and writing in his little notebook. "The Father and Jesus the Son both care much for us, don't they?" he said.

"Yes, and Jesus loved to speak of His Father, teaching others to pray 'Our Father' in what we call the Lord's Prayer.

"Now let's find the Gospel of Matthew—Matthew 7:7-11. Jesus was teaching His disciples and the crowds of people out on a hillside. Priest Peter, would you?"

" 'Ask, and it shall be given you; seek, and ye shall find; knock, and it shall be opened unto you: for every one that asketh receiveth; and he that seeketh findeth; and to him that knocketh it shall be opened. Or what man is there of you, whom if his son ask bread, will he give him a stone? Or if he ask a fish, will he give him a serpent? If ye then, being evil, know how to give good gifts unto your children, how much more shall your Father which is in heaven give good things to them that ask him?' ''

"Thank you, Priest Peter. Just think of it! Jesus says, 'How much *more* will your Father which is in heaven give good things to them that ask Him!' We just read in James that every good and perfect gift comes from the Father.

"Let's read more about what Jesus said concerning His Father—Matthew 6:25-33. This passage is part of the same sermon from which we just read. Brother Thomas, would you?"

'' 'Therefore I say unto you, Take no thought for your life, what ye shall eat, or what ye shall drink; nor yet for your body, what ye shall put on. Is not the life more than meat, and the body than raiment? Behold the fowls of the air: for they sow not, neither do they reap, nor gather into barns; yet your heavenly Father feedeth them. Are ye not much better than they? Which of you by taking thought can add one cubit unto his stature? And why take ye thought for raiment? Consider the lilies of the field, how they grow; they toil not, neither do they spin: And yet I say unto you, That even Solomon in all his glory was not arrayed like one of these. Wherefore, if God so clothe the grass of the field, which to day is, and to morrow is cast into the oven, shall he not much more clothe you, O ye of little faith? Therefore take no thought, saying, What shall we eat? or, What shall we drink? or, Wherewithal shall we be clothed? (For after all these things do the Gentiles seek:) for your heavenly Father knoweth that ye have need of all these things. But seek ye first the kingdom of God, and his righteousness; and all these things shall be added unto you.' "

Priest Shemaiah smiled. "What a wonderful Father! He's *my* Father!"

The other priest nodded. "And He's *mine,* too!"

"Jesus called Him not only *Father* but also *God.* Do you remember the story of how on resurrection morning Mary Magdalene talked with Jesus in the garden by the tomb?

"John 20:17 tells us about it. 'Jesus saith unto her, Touch me not; for I am not yet ascended to my Father: but go to my brethren and say unto them, I ascend unto my Father, and your Father; and to my God, and your God.'

"When He said, 'Touch me not,' He was really saying, 'Do not hold on to Me to detain Me.'

"It's a wonderful thought that our God is our Father! He cares for us, providing all our needs. And He is God—the one God, the Creator who made us, the God whom we worship."

Shemaiah sighed deeply. "It's good, so good. I love this Book. I wish I had had one long ago."

"So do I," his brother-in-law agreed. "I used to think that the real Bible was written only in the language of the liturgy. That every religious work in our current language was heresy. And I was sure these Bibles were heretical books. When you gave them out I thought maybe you were a Roman Catholic. I didn't like that either."

"No," I responded, "I am not a Roman Catholic, but I have a number of friends who are Catholics who love God very much and they read their Bibles."

"I'm glad God is my Father," Priest Shemaiah

repeated with a faraway look in his eyes. "I was an orphan. The high priest reared me. Now I must lean heavily on God, my heavenly Father. I don't know what my family is going to do for food. The custom is for the church members to bring food from their gardens or farms or shops to the priests. Also, we priests receive some land from the church to farm, but we don't have enough to support a family. Already most people have quit bringing food to our house because I'm not working as a priest at this time. But you just read what Jesus said: 'Your heavenly Father knows what you need.' "

"He not only knows—He will do something about it," I assured him. " 'All these things will be added unto you,' He promises. Maybe you'd like to read one more verse—Philippians 4:19."

Shemaiah read, " 'My God shall supply all your need according to his riches in glory by Christ Jesus.' Wonderful! Wonderful!" he exclaimed, turning to his brother-in-law. "We don't have to worry because we have God our Father with us. We know it. Others don't have to know our secrets!" he said with a chuckle that carried a tinge of sacred awe. (I would see his mannerism many times in the future. It seemed to reveal his deep delight at having secrets with the most high God when all about him his world seemed to be cracking.)

TALKING TO THE FATHER

The next time Priest Shemaiah came his face glowed. As he sat down he exclaimed, "I'm so happy, so happy! Just to think that Jesus has forgiven all my sins. Jesus! *My* Saviour! And just to think that God the Father loves us just as Jesus does! And I don't have to confess to a soul father. Oh, I do like going alone to Jesus and confessing! To lie down at night—every night—with my sins all forgiven. I don't have to wait for an appointment with a priest. What joy! What joy!

"Those people who used to come to me to confess—they are so happy! Free, joyous forgiveness direct from our Saviour!" His eyes sparkled with delight as the dancing flames in the fireplace seemed to reflect his mood. "Sometimes I meet some of them at the market. They are rejoicing in Jesus' forgiveness. Whenever I have an opportunity I tell them more about the forgiveness of Jesus and how He changes us if we let Him."

The priest let out a long sigh and shook his head. "Why did I have to wait all these years to find this out? Think of all the time I've wasted for myself and others. Think of all the things I've taught them that aren't true. But I thank God that He has brought His Word to me and that He has given this bright light to shine on my path.

"Tonight I want you to show me how to talk to our Father in heaven. Yes, I know the Lord's Prayer, but teach me to *talk* to my Father."

After our evening prayer I suggested that he turn to Philippians 4:6, " 'Be careful for nothing; but in every

41

thing by prayer and supplication with thanksgiving let your requests be made known unto God. And the peace of God, which passeth all understanding, shall keep your hearts and minds through Christ Jesus.' "

"Priest Shemaiah," I said, "the expression 'Be careful for nothing' means to have no anxious thought—no worry. Instead of worrying, we can make our requests known to God. But we should do this with thanksgiving, for it is God who gives us every blessing we have. 'By prayer and supplication' reminds us to address God with humble entreaty.

"So the apostle Paul is telling us several points about prayer. Do not worry, but express gratitude; approach and entreat our Father from a sense of humility, and tell Him our requests. True humility will allow Him to answer as He sees best.

"Then what happens? Instead of worry, His peace will keep our hearts and minds from succumbing to despair and panic."

"That is good—very good!" the priest agreed. "Can you explain Mark 11:24? It says, 'What things soever ye desire, when ye pray, believe that ye receive them, and ye shall have them.' Does this mean that God gives us everything we ask for?"

"Yes and no. In one way it means that, but in another, it does not. The passage is really speaking of believing, of having faith. If we have the right kind of faith, we will pray as Jesus taught us to pray, 'Thy will be done in earth, as it is in heaven.' This is really a prayer of surrender. When we pray in this way, it means that we seek for our desires to be in harmony with those of our heavenly Father. So if we want something, we will ask Him, but we will not request something we know to be contrary to His will.

"Since we may not know what His will is, we must leave room for Him to show us. Then He will answer our prayer according to what He, in His infinite wisdom, sees best, while we, in turn, can rejoice that He has answered our prayer. God always gives us the best if we let Him.

"Would you like to read verse 25 now?"

" 'And when ye stand praying, forgive, if ye have ought against any: that your Father also which is in heaven may forgive you your trespasses.' "

"Forgiveness is another condition for praying," I explained. "We must forgive if we want God's forgiveness. An unforgiving person is really unable himself to accept forgiveness from God. He will have no peace in his heart, since anger and resentment drive away the peace that comes from a sense of total forgiveness by God. If we really experience God's forgiveness, it will flow out of us to others.

"Let's look at a promise God makes to those who ask and believe. Brother Thomas, would you like to read James 1:5, 6?"

" 'If any of you lack wisdom, let him ask of God, that giveth to all men liberally, and upbraideth not; and it shall be given him' " the translator read.

Brother Thomas paused. "God gives wisdom generously without reproach if we ask Him," he then commented. "He surely is a wonderful Father! It goes on to say, 'But let him ask in faith, nothing wavering. For he that wavereth is like a wave of the sea driven with the wind and tossed.' "

"God is speaking here of faith again," Priest Shemaiah observed. "If we ask, but leave the results to God, aren't we showing a lack of faith?"

"No, we can ask in faith, knowing that all things

are possible with God. We waver when we doubt His love and His ability to answer us. But when we believe that He is really able to do even more than we ask and that He will do us only good, then He will give us all the wisdom that we need. If we lack faith, we can ask Him for that, too."

The priest looked up from his Bible. "This means that God will give me wisdom to know what to say and do when I go to church on Sundays? And He will help me to know how to answer questions? Well, I surely do need much wisdom." He smiled as he leaned back and rubbed his forehead. "But what about sinning? Does God answer prayer even when we sin?"

As he straightened up, a frown crept across his face. "You know, I find myself doing wrong sometimes. There are situations where I'm impatient—almost angry—before I even realize it. This happens especially when I see priests following me around town to spy on what I'm doing. I ask God to forgive me, and I believe He does. But will He really hear me pray about other things?"

"Well, let's look at James 5:16: 'Confess your faults one to another, and pray one for another, that ye may be healed. The effectual fervent prayer of a righteous man availeth much.'

"This says to confess your faults to one another. It does not mean to disclose them to a priest, though. We have already learned that we confess our sins to Jesus. But when we have wronged a person—be he priest or layman—we need to admit it and ask his forgiveness. Then we may pray for other things—in the situation of this verse, for healing.

"It goes on to speak of a *righteous* person. When

we have confessed our sins we are cleansed. God counts us as righteous, and hears and answers our prayers.

"Psalm 66:18 says, 'If I regard iniquity in my heart, the Lord will not hear me.' That is, if we hang on to sin, if we love it, cherish it, God does not hear us. This does not mean that we are lost should we ever yield to temptation. If we do, we need to confess this to God and ask Him to give us strength to overcome it. If our thoughts are wrong we must ask Him to forgive us and to keep us from falling.

"This does not mean that we will not be tempted. For example, when you see these priests that the church court appointed to follow you, you may get really angry and say wrong things. But God will take care of this in His own time. Meanwhile, He calls you to be a witness for Him."

"A witness?" Shemaiah looked puzzled.

OUR HIGH-PRIEST GUARDIAN

"Yes, a witness," I affirmed. "Brother Thomas, would you read 1 Peter 2:19-25 while we follow?"

" 'For this is thankworthy, if a man for conscience toward God endure grief, suffering wrongfully. For what glory is it, if, when ye be buffeted for your faults, ye shall take it patiently? but if, when ye do well, and suffer for it, ye take it patiently, this is acceptable with God. For even hereunto were ye called: because

Christ also suffered for us, leaving us an example, that ye should follow his steps: who did no sin, neither was guile found in his mouth: who, when he was reviled, reviled not again; when he suffered, he threatened not; but committed himself to him that judgeth righteously: who his own self bare our sins in his own body on the tree, that we, being dead to sins, should live unto righteousness: by whose stripes ye were healed. For ye were as sheep going astray; but are now returned unto the Shepherd and Bishop of your souls.'

"This is a very interesting passage," the translator remarked when he finished.

"What do you find interesting?" I inquired. "It was actually directed to servants—slaves."

"The writer of this letter, Peter, was the one who stood by the fire warming himself on that Thursday night before the crucifixion. He saw the church leaders reviling Jesus. He saw that Jesus did not insult them, that He didn't retaliate or make any threats, that He simply committed His case to the righteous Judge in heaven."

"It's a beautiful picture of our Saviour," I agreed.

"But why do we have to suffer just because Jesus did?" Priest Shemaiah seemed puzzled.

"There are several main reasons that Jesus permits us to suffer, though He is not responsible for the suffering. He is not saying, 'I suffered for you, so now I'm going to make you suffer so you can feel sorry for me.' Never would He do that.

"But He has chosen to bring good out of suffering."

"How?"

"Suffering helps us to perfect character if we trust

46

ourselves with the Saviour. During suffering it is our privilege to see and experience the deep, tender love of God in a way that we often fail to appreciate when all is going well.

"Also, suffering can teach us to lean our whole weight on God.

"Further, out of such experiences we can witness to God's power to comfort, to strengthen, to provide. We can demonstrate to others that God can and does keep us from falling into bitterness, unforgiveness, anger, and revenge. Through us people can see what God is like, and because of this, many will want to follow Him.

"I like the way that the apostle Peter says that before conversion we are as straying sheep, but we who are Christians now have returned to the Shepherd and Bishop of our souls. That word *bishop* means overseer, or guardian."

Priest Shemaiah's face was radiant. "This means, then, that when these priests follow me I have an opportunity to develop character like Jesus had if I trust Him to help me. Is that right?"

"Yes."

"Also that Christ wants me to witness to them what *He* is like, by acting like Christ. Is that it?"

I nodded.

"Then Jesus is my bishop—that is, my overseer—and my guardian."

Suddenly, as if a dark shadow had swept it away, the light left the man's face. Brother Thomas and I waited. He hung his head and pulled at the fringe on his blanket. Staring into the fireplace, he said, "I forget so easily. I'll go out tomorrow and see them following me. And before I have a chance to think I'll be angry inside. *Then* what will God do for me? What can I pray to Him *then?*" His voice was pleading.

"Pray as the apostle Paul did," I suggested, "when he found himself standing alone." I turned to 2 Timothy 4:16-18: " 'No man stood with me, but all men forsook me: I pray God that it may not be laid to their charge. Notwithstanding the Lord stood with me, and strengthened me. . . . And the Lord shall deliver me from every evil work.' "

The priest repeated, " 'The Lord shall deliver me from every evil work.' No man stood with me, but the Lord stood with me."

"Yes, the Lord will deliver you from every evil work—from the spies and from your anger toward them. He is standing by you—your great high priest. If you ask Him He will deliver you. We need to lean on Him, to study His Word and pray, to keep close enough to Him so that He can protect us.

"Yet in learning to do this, we might fall at times. In 1 John 2:1 the apostle John says, 'My little children, these things write I unto you, that ye sin not. And if any man sin, we have an advocate with the Father, Jesus Christ the righteous.'

"So we need to confess to God. And if we do wrong to our fellowmen, we need to ask their forgiveness—even if they committed the greater sin against us."

"Why should we ask their forgiveness when they are to blame?" Priest Shemaiah protested.

"Because we are professing to be children of God. If we leave others with the impression that God acts as we do when we are angry, they will not receive a correct picture of His character. We are to reveal the character of Jesus so that others will appreciate Him and follow Him.

"And there is another reason for asking their forgiveness. These people who have been hounding you, even though they are not acting as followers of Christ, nevertheless are His personal property. To do or say anything unChristlike to them is to make it much more difficult for God to bring them to Himself. Some of those who are—perhaps unwittingly—on Satan's side will someday recognize that they have been wrong in what they are doing and will join God's family and become trusting, obedient children."

The flames had nearly died, leaving a bed of crackling red coals in the fireplace.

The priest took up his notebook, in which he had written the Bible texts and the main ideas from each text. "Let's see now what we have said about talking to our heavenly Father." He read slowly from his notes: "Don't be anxious; trust God. Express thankfulness. Always pray 'Thy will be done.' Forgive others. Remember that God does not scold, but gives generously. Confess our faults to one another. Pray for one another. Do not cherish sin."

He looked up from the notebook at us. "Please pray that I'll never forget this. I have decided that I can speak to Him as I would to my own father. It's hard not to have a father. You know I mentioned before that I was an orphan and the high priest took me as his child when I was young. Now he is discouraged with me. Things are not as they used to be. But I'm so thankful that I have a heavenly Father who cares."

THE SAINTS

The next evening Priest Shemaiah knocked on my door. "Please, sister, may Priest Peter and I come tomorrow evening to study? We have many questions," he explained in a whisper. "We don't want to wait until Sunday."

"Yes, come," I whispered back.

As he turned to leave, I could see the smile on his face by the light of the half-moon. "Thank you," he murmured as he hurried down the steps. I watched him round the corner of the house where dewy roses hung over the fence.

The next morning I asked Brother Thomas if he could come in the evening to translate. When he said he couldn't come, I contacted Brother Adam, a good teacher and an excellent teacher of Bible.

That evening all three men arrived at the same time. Martha studied in the adjoining dining room, ears atune with curiosity.

"We have many, many questions tonight," Shemaiah began. "You know I told you that the provincial patriarch is returning to hear my answers. Time is passing. There is much I must learn before he arrives. Can you help us?"

"Well, we can study and pray about it all. Why don't we pray now?"

After the prayer Priest Shemaiah unfolded a sheet of paper. "Here are our questions for tonight. Who are the saints? What does Saint Mary do? The Bible speaks of tradition—what does it mean? What about fasting—should we do it for forty days? We were baptized when we were infants. What did that really mean? Is sprinkling a good form of baptism? Is it better to be a monk than to be married? What about crucifying ourselves? Do we have to hate our mothers and fathers to follow Jesus? What does it mean to take up your cross and follow Him? Who are the angels? What are works of the flesh? What does it mean when it says 'Love not the world'? That's the last question on my list," he said as he nervously folded the paper in half, then folded it again and slid it into his pocket. "But I have more that I've not written."

"All of that tonight?" I asked with a smile.

"As much as we can cover," he nodded with a serious look on his face.

"Well, which question shall we take first?"

"The saints. You see, we were speaking last time about praying to the Father. Priest Peter and I have been reading our Bibles, trying to find out about venerating the saints. Are we supposed to implore them to intercede for us? Are we to try to imitate them?

"In our church we have thirty days in each month. On each day we venerate a different saint. But 1 John 2:1 says, 'If any man sin, we have an advocate with the Father, Jesus Christ the righteous.' And then we discovered the text in Hebrews 7:25 that we are to 'come unto God by him, seeing he ever liveth to make intercession for them.' Back in chapter 4:14-16 we found that 'we have a great high priest, that is passed into the heavens, Jesus the Son of God.' "

Shemaiah leaned back and sighed.

"So what is the problem?" I asked.

"Well, it says *Jesus* is our advocate. It says *He* saves anyone who comes to God by *Him*. Jesus is our great high priest who ever liveth to make intercession for us. It says to come boldly to the throne of grace. That's God's throne, isn't it?''

"It looks as if you have been studying your Bible. Let's look at John 16:23, 24. Priest Peter, will you read it for us?''

" 'Verily, verily, I say unto you, Whatsoever ye shall ask the Father in my name, he will give it you. Hitherto have ye asked nothing in my name: ask, and ye shall receive, that your joy may be full.' ''

"So once again," I observed, "Scripture tells us to ask the Father directly in the name of Jesus.''

"Is there any place where it says in the Bible that we should ask the saints to intercede for us?" Priest Shemaiah inquired.

"I have read my Bible through several times but have never found such a passage," I replied. "Have you found one?''

The priests shook their heads. "We have looked for days," Shemaiah said, "but there is nothing.''

"Is there any place that says we should venerate the saints?" Peter asked.

"Have you found any?" I questioned.

"No.''

"I haven't either.''

Priest Shemaiah had another question. "Well, who are the saints? What do they do?''

"I'll let you answer that, Brother Adam," I said.

"The word *saint* is translated from one word in the New Testament and from two in the Old Testament describing a thing or a person that is 'separated, set apart, holy,' '' he explained.

"The Scriptures, particularly the writings of Paul, use the word *saint* to describe the people who have

52

committed themselves to be Christians—to be God's children. Let's look at 1 Corinthians 1:2: 'Unto the church of God which is at Corinth, to them that are sanctified in Christ Jesus, called to be saints, with all that in every place call upon the name of Jesus Christ our Lord, both theirs and ours.'

"These people are sanctified—set apart or separate in Christ Jesus. In the Greek, *saint* and *sanctified* come from the same root word. The Greek word means *separate, holy*. If we are separate from the world—if we are in Jesus Christ, *His* holy people, calling upon *His* name—we are saints.

"We can see this clearly in 1 Corinthians 6:1. Let's read it. 'Dare any of you, having a matter against another, go to law before the unjust, and not before the saints?' The Greek word for *unjust* means also *unrighteous*. Shall God's holy people go to unrighteous men to settle their problems?

"These and other texts make it clear that according to the Bible a follower of God is a saint."

Priest Shemaiah still seemed unsatisfied. "But aren't some followers better than others? Some have done much more good for people and for God than others have. Don't they deserve veneration?"

Adam smiled. "Here is an interesting passage in Ephesians 6:18, 19. Paul is speaking of how we wrestle against Satan and his power and he cautions us to put on the Christian armor. Then with all this he adds, 'Praying always with all prayer and supplication in the Spirit, and watching thereunto with all perseverance and supplication for all saints; and for me, that utterance may be given unto me, that I may open my mouth boldly, to make known the mystery of the gospel.' Paul is telling the Ephesian Christians to pray *for all saints.* He even wants them to pray for him."

I was glad that Brother Adam could help me with some of the answers. He continued to explain, "Nowhere does Scripture tell us to venerate saints— that is, God's holy people, those who have accepted Jesus. We ought to honor our parents and show proper respect for those in authority in the church and government, as well as the aged, but not to venerate some of them as more unselfish, self-deny-ing, or obedient than others, or as having special influence with God."

"So . . ." Priest Peter reflected, "God does not expect us to have special days for the saints?"

"That is what the Bible indicates," Adam replied.

Brother Shemaiah turned to his brother-in-law and said slowly, "This surely changes things for me. On many of the saints' days we can't plow or cut wood. Sometimes we spend two or three days in church, besides Sundays, to venerate the saints. I used to participate in those services when they allowed me to help. But I don't think I could ever do it again. No, I don't think I could do it again."

"I feel that way too," Priest Peter replied, "but I want to think about it some more."

HOLY PEOPLE

Priest Shemaiah remained silent, thinking. Brother Adam casually turned the pages of his New Testament until his eyes fell on Philippians 1:1.

"Here's an interesting text," he said, breaking the silence. "Paul wrote this from Rome where he was a prisoner awaiting trial for preaching about Christ: 'Paul and Timotheus, the servants of Jesus Christ, to all the saints in Christ Jesus which are at Philippi, with the bishops and deacons.' Now that is a beautiful way of stating it! 'To all the saints . . . with the bishops and deacons.' If I'd been a member there I'd have been one of those saints, for I'm not a deacon or a bishop, but just an ordinary follower of Christ."

"What did those church members have to do to be saints—to be holy, or at least to be called holy?" Priest Peter asked him.

"Verses 1 and 6 tell some of the answer. You notice, in verse 1, the saints are 'in Christ Jesus,' and verse 6 says, 'He which hath begun a good work in you will perform it.' It is *Christ* who does the good work in His saints.

"In chapter 2:13, Paul declares, 'It is God which worketh in you both to will and to do of his good pleasure.' We are in Christ and He begins His work in us when we decide to be His followers—His children. If we continue to accept His leading, to repent when He convicts us of sin in our lives, to confess our sin and to accept His forgiveness, He will finish His work in us. He gives repentance. He helps us to confess. He forgives.

55

"Hebrews 11 gives the names of many of God's children in the Old Testament who became faithful, holy people by the grace of God. But God did not want us who live now to become discouraged in the Christian life. So the discussion continues in chapter 12:1. Priest Shemaiah, will you read for us?"

" 'Wherefore seeing we also are compassed about with so great a cloud of witnesses, let us lay aside every weight, and the sin which doth so easily beset us, and let us run with patience the race that is set before us.' "

"The cloud of witnesses who attested to God's power to change their lives were those mentioned in Hebrews 11," Brother Adam explained. "Then we are told to lay aside every weight—everything that hinders us from being what we should be—and the sin that tangles us up and trips us as we journey to heaven. It is our part to lay these aside. God will not force us to. Each day we must come to Him and choose to follow Him, to leave off all unchristian thoughts and actions, and to live like His children.

"But that is not enough. We must run with patience—perseverance, endurance—but we'll never make it with just that. Sister, will you please read verse 2 for us?"

" 'Looking unto Jesus the author and finisher of our faith; who for the joy that was set before him endured the cross, despising the shame, and is set down at the right hand of the throne of God.' "

"This passage," Pastor Adam said, "is full of helpful thoughts for Christians. Where does it say that Jesus is?"

"At the right hand of the throne of God," Priest Peter replied.

"Yes, do you remember that we read in Hebrews 4:14-16 that Jesus is our high priest who ascended into heaven, and that we were told to come boldly to the throne of grace?

"Hebrews 12:2 describes Jesus as the author, or pioneer, or the one who began our faith."

Priest Shemaiah had a question. "You mean we don't have any faith of our own?"

"No, if we read Romans 12:3, we find that it is God that gives every man a measure of faith."

"Then with that faith and grace," Shemaiah said, "we can do good works that gain merit. When we've done enough good things, then God will give us more help—isn't that right?"

"Not quite right," Brother Adam responded. "God gives us faith. Then we learn that God loved the world so much that He gave His only Son that whoever *believes* in Him should not perish, but have eternal life. Thus God is the *author*—the beginner of our faith. He is its *giver*, and He also provides us a *Person* in whom we can believe. Our part then is to decide whether we will or will not believe."

"But," Priest Peter asked with a thoughtful frown, "when we believe, then we repent—doesn't that give us some merit with God?"

"No, repentance comes from God. Let's turn to Acts 5:31. It is speaking of Jesus, who is now at the throne of God. The apostle Peter and other apostles commented, 'Him [Jesus] hath God exalted with his right hand to be a Prince and a Saviour, for to give repentance to Israel, and forgiveness of sins.'

"So repentance comes as a gift from Jesus. When we do repent, He forgives, and that is also a gift. Besides that, *He* gives faith, and eternal life.

"If we feel that we need more faith, we can pray, 'Lord, I believe; help thou mine unbelief' [the prayer to Jesus by the father of the boy possessed by a demon].

"Only Jesus' death on the cross provides forgiveness and cleansing. 'The blood of Jesus Christ . . . cleanseth us from all sin,' 1 John 1:7 tells us."

"Put it like this," I said, "God gave—Jesus gave—faith, repentance, forgiveness, cleansing, and eternal life. All of these are gifts. We cannot in any way earn them or make ourselves worthy to receive them.

"Let's turn to Romans 6:23. 'The wages of sin is death; but the gift of God is eternal life through Jesus Christ our Lord.'

"Eternal life is a gift. We do not earn it, but we have it when we accept Jesus as our Saviour and Lord."

"Is this the way God's people become holy?" Priest Shemaiah asked, shaking his head in wonder.

"Will you read Hebrews 13:12? That will answer your question, I believe," Brother Adam responded.

" 'Wherefore Jesus also, that he might sanctify the people with his own blood, suffered without the gate,' " the priest read.

"How, then, are people sanctified, made holy?" Brother Adam asked.

"By the blood of Jesus," Shemaiah replied.

"Yes, He suffered on the cross—outside the gate of the city of Jerusalem, that He might make us holy. Now let's look at Hebrews 12:1, 2. It tells us that we should throw off everything that hinders us—we do this by using the faith God gives us, using His gift of repentance and forgiveness—and run with endurance in our race to heaven. This is not a competition where only one can win. All may triumph in this race.

"But the only way we can be successful is to fix our eyes on Jesus, who begins our faith and finishes or perfects it. As we move along He teaches us to trust in Him more and more. He changes us. Along the way He says we are sanctified, holy, because He covers us with His own righteousness."

Priest Shemaiah turned to his brother-in-law. "Did you ever hear any of this before?" he asked.

"No, I never did."

"To think that it is Jesus who makes us holy—not what *we* do!" Shemaiah reflected.

"And it's a *gift!*" Priest Peter added with a pleased smile.

"We—*we* ordinary people—are called to be saints, holy. It's almost too much to think about!" Shemaiah shook his head in wonder. "Oh, I love Jesus—more and more and more! And I do love this Book! Why did I have to wait so many years to learn this!"

CROSS, FLESH, WORLD

Priest Shemaiah stood and stretched. "Are you going home *now?*" Priest Peter asked. "We've only started on that list of questions that you read!"

"No. I just need to walk around and think a little," Shemaiah replied as he stretched again and put a chunk of wood in the fire. "It's so much to think about. Saints. Holy people. God makes His people holy if they let Him. He gives us faith, repentance, forgiveness, holiness, eternal life. How wonderful!

"Yet now, a month before Christmas, already pilgrims are beginning their journey to the sacred churches where our people long to earn merit with God. Just this morning I saw several very old women stumbling along as they walked barefoot. When I spoke to them they leaned on their staffs. They feel that they will have a better chance of reaching heaven if they make this journey, with all its hardships. Old clothes. No food. No money. Asking for bread along the way. Sleeping in the forest on the cold ground. Trying so hard to be sure that God will give them eternal life. Searching for peace. Always hoping, yet afraid. Oh, sister! Thousands of people will walk hundreds of miles across the mountains. Through the deserts. Hungry. Thirsty. Hoping that God will have mercy on them! Sister, sister! And to think that I taught my people to do that!" He leaned against the brick fireplace and stared at the wall.

Priest Peter sighed, "And I have taught them too. How could we have been so wrong!"

"Sister," Shemaiah said with tears in his eyes, "you told us a few weeks ago that you and some others plan to take many Bibles to those holy churches at Christmas. You said you'd be glad to have me go along and help. Now I don't know what I'll be getting into—dressed in priest's clothes and helping heretics give out books—but I have decided that I am really going. My brother-in-law has agreed that he will stay and take care of my farm while I am gone. He'll look after my wife and children."

Peter smiled and nodded.

"Yes, I'll go," Priest Shemaiah continued. "Sister, do you need me to help arrange transportation?"

"Oh, I'd be glad if you could do that," I replied.

"I can, by God's help. I know I can," he said. "But don't let the people around here know yet that I'm going. I wish they'd not know until I return."

"That's right," his brother-in-law agreed.

"Let's get back to questions," Shemaiah said as he sat down. "I have many more now—about keeping the law, since you said God finishes the work in us. But let's wait for that and finish my list first.

"About crucifying ourselves. You say we can't make ourselves holy and we read that it is *Christ's* blood that makes us holy. What does Galatians 5:24 mean?"

"Will you read it for us?" I asked. Brother Adam had nodded for me to take over. We enjoyed helping each other as a team.

Priest Shemaiah turned the pages and read, " 'And they that are Christ's have crucified the flesh with the affections and lusts.' And there are other similar texts—Romans 8:13 and Matthew 16:24-26. Also 1 John 2:15, and . . ."

"Wait!" I said. "Don't go so fast. Let's work with these before you add any more. What troubles you about them?"

"The Bible says we should crucify the flesh with the affections and the lusts," he replied. "That we should deny ourselves and take up our cross. Whoever saves his life shall lose it. It tells us to 'love not the world, neither the things that are in the world.' And it speaks of the lust of the flesh, the lust of the eyes, and the pride of life." Leaning back, he sighed deeply. Then looking at me with a helpless

61

expression, he sighed again and shook his head. He waited in silence.

"Brother Adam, I'll let you work on this," I said, smiling.

Let's turn to Galatians 2:20," he suggested. "Priest Peter, will you read it?"

After the priest finished Adam said, "Now, let's analyze this verse.

" 'I am crucified with Christ:
   nevertheless I live;
   yet not I [live],
   but Christ liveth in me:
   and the life which I now live in the flesh
   I live by the faith of the Son of God,
       who loved me,
       and gave himself for me.'

"Paul says he's *crucified,* but he *lives.* Yet it's not *he* who lives, but *Christ* lives in him. He speaks of the life he *now* lives as coming by the faith of the Son of God. His new life is still lived *in the flesh.*" He paused a moment. "Now if his new life came by faith in the Son of God, what was the source of his old life?"

"Faith in or following something besides Christ," Peter replied.

"That's true. Paul said, 'I am crucified.' He crucified everything that he had trusted in: himself, his pleasures, his desires. The apostle crucified his dependence upon everything except God—everything that was contrary to faith in Jesus.

"But he did not kill his physical body—his physical flesh. He states clearly that after he was crucified he still lived a life in the flesh. And he did it by faith in Jesus, who loved him and gave Himself for him—for Paul.

"In other words, Paul put all his confidence—his hope of salvation—in Jesus, not in himself, not in anyone or anything else.

"Let's look at Romans 6:11. Shemaiah, you may read this time."

" 'Likewise reckon ye also yourselves to be dead indeed unto sin, but alive unto God . . .' " He glanced up at us.

"Reckon yourselves to be dead to sin, but *alive* unto God because of Jesus," Brother Adam explained to him.

"We have turned around. No longer do we let sin reign in us. We have a new King—Jesus—and do not obey the inclinations to sin. Instead we crucify them.

"But we accomplish all of this by accepting God's gifts of faith, repentance, confession, and forgiveness. Jesus' death for us has made this possible for us.

"Paul contrasts fleshly desires with those of individuals who have determined to follow Christ—individuals who are spiritual or filled with the Spirit of Christ.

"But when he speaks of works of the flesh or fleshly desires, he is not referring to the need for sleep or food, a point that is obvious when we read Galatians 5:19-21."

Priest Peter located the passage. " 'Now the works of the flesh are manifest, which are these; Adultery, fornication, uncleanness, lasciviousness, idolatry, witchcraft, hatred, variance, emulations, wrath, strife, seditions, heresies, envyings, murders, drunkenness, revellings, and such like: of the which I tell you before, as I have also told you in time past, that they which do such things shall not inherit the kingdom of God.' "

"Here," Brother Adam observed, "Paul depicts those who follow the desires of the flesh, the desires of those who depend on everything else but their Creator. These are the lusts that we must crucify. But to accomplish this we must yield ourselves to God's life, must accept His Spirit in our lives.

"When the Spirit comes in, He brings—well, let's read on in Galatians 5. Verses 22-24: 'But the fruit of the Spirit is love, joy, peace, longsuffering, gentleness, goodness, faith, meekness, temperance: against such there is no law. And they that are Christ's have crucified the flesh with the affections and lusts.'

"The flesh that we need to crucify, then, is our sinful nature, not our physical bodies. We must put to death those affections and desires not in keeping with the character of Christ. Then we live a new life—the life Christ desires us to live, the one Christ gives us power to live."

Priest Shemaiah leaned back with a relaxed smile. "So crucifying the flesh isn't walking barefoot on hot sand or sleeping on the bare ground. It's crucifying sin and accepting Jesus' new life instead. I never knew that before—never!" he exclaimed.

Then he grew serious again. "What about denying ourselves, taking up our cross and following Him?" he asked.

Brother Adam nodded. "It takes a great deal of self-denial to allow the Spirit of Christ to produce the fruits of the Spirit. At every point we must crucify selfishness and pride. But it is the only way we can follow Jesus. We carry our cross with us as we follow Him."

Priest Shemaiah fingered a brass cross that he always had with him. "We priests say that the passage means that we should take up a cross like this and carry it. That isn't what it is speaking about?''

"It doesn't sound that way," Adam replied. "It's talking about denying oneself and following Jesus which, as we have seen, is done by crucifying fleshly works and attitudes. It's giving Jesus a chance to give us new life. And it's repentance, continual repentance. That is, a daily turning away from sin to accept the righteousness of Jesus. However, it does not mean continual sorrow over sins that are past and forgiven.''

"I can see that," Priest Peter observed. "But what about losing our lives for Christ's sake?''

"It may be that as we follow Jesus we will find ourselves at a point where we have to decide between Him and something or someone else. Jesus promises here that if that happens and we choose Him, that even if we die because of the decision, He will give us eternal life.''

"So," asked Shemaiah, "it's not saying we should starve ourselves until we die, or work so hard for Jesus that we become sick and perhaps die?''

"No, God is a loving God, as well as a just God," Brother Adam responded. "He wants His children to be happy, though He knows that they will sometimes face heavy trials and temptations.''

"But what about 'Love not the world, neither the things that are in the world'? You know that hermit who lives alone in the little house by the church? The man never goes to market—a friend does it for him. He told me he has lived alone for seven years so that he will not love the world or anything in it. Because there's no one to lie to, he's not tempted to lie. The absence of a wife, children, or anybody else around keeps him from getting angry. And since people bring him food, he has no impulse to steal. Locked up away from the world, he finds it's easy to be good. The monks in the monasteries do the same thing." Priest Shemaiah was troubled.

"We have already seen that Paul said that the life he lived, he lived by faith in the Son of God," Adam replied. "And we read how it is *God* who works in us to change us.

"When God says not to love the world or the things in it, He is speaking of anything in opposition to God or anything that leads us away from Him, such as clinging to worldly people or hanging on to material things. We dishonor Him when we put His created works ahead of Him who is the Creator. Rather than to do this, we should put God first in everything and thank Him for all that He has made for us. Never should we allow anything else to become supreme in our lives.

"John makes this clear in 1 John 2:16: 'For all that is in the world, the lust of the flesh, and the lust of the eyes, and the pride of life, is not of the Father, but is of the world.' 'Lust of the flesh' (craving to do evil), 'lust of the eyes' (looking at and enjoying sin even without participating in it), and the 'pride of life' (putting ourselves and our desires above God)—all these things make us 'of the *world*,' as opposed to the way of God our Father.

"Further, in Colossians 3:2 God urges us, 'Set your affection on things above, not on things on the earth.' Notice that in verse 17 and following, God speaks to wives, husbands, children, fathers, servants, and masters, telling them all how to live together in peace and joy. He does not suggest that they go into isolation. The whole chapter speaks of what people will be like when they set their affections on heavenly things. By doing so, they live better in this world. They have crucified the works of the flesh and live by the power of Christ. Now they love Him more than they love anyone else or anything else. He is in them, and they in Him, and thus they do love and help one another. A true Christian will love because Christ loves.''

It was nearly nine-thirty. Martha, who had been studying in the dining room, closed her books.

"What do you think of all this discussion, Martha?'' Shemaiah asked as he and his friend stood to leave.

"I found it very helpful,'' she replied.

"We should be going,'' he said. "Sister, may we come again tomorrow night?''

"I have another appointment tomorrow night. How about the following night?''

"We'll be here,'' he said with a smile.

PILGRIM PATIENT

That night as I lay in bed, staring out the window at the nearly full moon, many thoughts raced through my mind. Just that afternoon a barefoot monk, dressed in an old sheepskin, wooden beads around his neck, staff in one hand, brass cross in the other, had come as a patient to the clinic. A fine-looking man, he was happy to be on his way with other pilgrims. Already he had walked nearly a hundred miles, carrying his cross and following Jesus, as he explained to me. He told me he had never been married—he was living a spiritual life, not one in the flesh. Nor had he ever worked for a living—to do so would be loving the world. The monk was disciplining his mind to think only of God and spiritual things. The less he thought of his body, the better he would be.

"Spiritual things are what count," he said with a bright, quiet smile, and leaned back in his chair.

"What brings you here?" I had asked.

"I have a very bad cough."

"I noticed that. You can hardly speak. Where have you been sleeping?"

"Along the road."

"But it's December. The weather is cold."

"Jesus suffered, and I too must suffer," he replied. "I want to reach those churches. There is a heavy weight by one of them. All the pilgrims try to lift it. If they can, their sins are forgiven. But if they cannot, their sins remain unforgiven, and they will need to do more penance."

"But suppose some of those very old women cannot lift the weight? Then what?" I asked, crying inside for the woes of humankind all over the world.

"If their sins are forgiven, God will give them enough strength. But if they are not forgiven, they will need to work some more."

"What about God's holy Book? It says, 'If we confess our sins, he is faithful and just to forgive us our sins, and to cleanse us from all unrighteousness.' According to the Bible all you or those women need to do is to confess your sins to God and believe He forgives because He has said it."

"No, no," he replied firmly with a faint smile. "That is not the true gospel."

We talked for more than an hour. I gave him an injection and some pills for his cough, wondering why he had come to have me help his body get better since, according to his ideas, he should be subjecting it to mistreatment. But doubtless he was concerned that he might not have the strength to walk another ten days to the place where he could at last discover whether God had forgiven his sins.

Also, I had given him a Bible, which he promised to leave at a friend's house until he returned. Picking up his staff, he had headed out the door, after shaking my hand in deep gratitude.

I couldn't get that man off my mind as I lay there in the darkness praying. An owl in a distant tree cried out in its own melancholy way. Sitting in the blackness. Crying. I found myself crying too.

A priest came to my mind. "I ran away from home when I was 9 years old to become a priest," he had told me.

"You didn't ask your parents—or even tell them, or even say Goodbye?"

"No." He smiled happily.

"Were your parents unkind to you?"

"No. We had a good home. But the priests taught us that the ones who walk closest with God are those who hate their fathers and mothers. If we truly hated them, we would run away. So I did."

"Have you ever been home since?"

"No, it's about forty years since I last saw them."

"Have you ever sent a message to them?"

"No."

"Do they know where you are?"

"No."

"But Jesus didn't do that!" I exclaimed. "When He was dying on the cross, He arranged for the apostle John to look after His beloved mother."

"But it was Jesus who said we should hate our parents," the priest had answered quietly.

"But what about all the teachings of the New Testament where it speaks of loving members of the family—husbands, wives, children? There is not one place where it says that breaking up families makes people holy."

Unmoved, he had continued to smile.

I tossed and turned. The owl still called mournfully.

"They don't understand the New Testament. They just don't understand," I said to myself, wishing I could go to sleep.

"It could be put on a chart this way—" I was trying to think, but couldn't. Years later I made the chart.

All people are natural persons to begin with. They may become spiritual ones if they choose to.

Natural Person	Spiritual Person
A natural person is one who has been born once. He or she comes into the world with a sinful nature—a bent toward, an enjoyment of, sin. His motives consist of pleasing self, and he	A spiritual person has been born twice: first, the usual physical birth, and the second time, born of the Spirit. That is, he has come to realize, by God's convicting power, that he possesses nothing except

depends on himself or someone or something besides God.

God continually seeks to draw people from this state, trying to win them over to accept the second birth. Such persons often do many good things and can have an attractive appearance, though others of them become the basest of criminals. But no matter how good they may seem, they are still natural persons until they have accepted God into their lives and made Him the center of them.

as it comes from God. People depend upon Him for everything—life, air, food, water; physical, mental, and spiritual strength; repentance, forgiveness, cleansing, eternal life. The spiritual person has accepted Christ's sacrifice for sin and His Spirit in his life and walks in God's ways.

To be a spiritual person is not to deny the physical body or its normal physical needs. It is not to downgrade it in any way. Rather it is to recognize that God calls it His temple, where His Spirit dwells. Thus he must promote its health and well-being—to use it in God's work and to accomplish His commands.

The New Testament has a number of words that it can use in several ways. Bible writers took some of these words, using them to describe natural and spiritual people.

The Natural Person	The Spiritual Person
Natural man	Spiritual man
Walks after the flesh	Walks after the Spirit
Worldly	Heavenly or godly
Unrighteous	Righteous
Unclean	Clean
Sinful	Holy
Unsanctified	Sanctified
Sinner	Saint
Old man	New man
Lost	Found or saved
In darkness	In light
Unfaithful	Faithful
Unbeliever	Believer
Unjust	Just
Carnally minded	Spiritually minded
Unredeemed	Redeemed
In bondage	In freedom
Servant or slave to sin	Son (occasionally servant of God)
Dead	Living
Child of darkness	Child of light
In spirit of error	In spirit of truth
Clothed in rags	Clothed in robes of righteousness

Note: The words translated *flesh, fleshly, carnal,* and *carnally* all come from the same Greek root word, *sarx.* The New Testament writers use all of them to indicate a *state* of a person or a *person* himself rather than any *part* of a person. When Paul employs these words in connection with man's spiritual condition—his relationship with God—he intends them to show man's sinful condition, his separation from God. The Greeks did not employ *sarx* when they described what they *thought* was man's nature—a body and a spirit. Rather they used the word *soma*. (Paul does not teach the concept of two separate parts of a human being—body and spirit.)

FAMILY HATRED

The next morning I found myself pondering more and more Bible texts. Every available moment that day and the following one I spent searching for answers to questions that I was sure Priest Shemaiah would bring. I was amazed at how the Bible explains itself if one prays to God for guidance and really searches its pages. The priest was learning this too.

Tuesday night the men arrived again. I was glad that Brother Adam could come again since Brother Thomas couldn't.

"I want to know about your families," I said. "How are things at home?"

"My wife is sick," Priest Peter replied.

"I would like to go and see her" I commented.

"No," he said quietly. "If someone sees, it could be bad for us. So far no one knows that I am coming here. But if anyone finds out, we'll be in trouble."

"I understand. But you know I am willing. I'll surely pray for her."

"My children are all well. We are happy," he

finished.

"And you, Priest Shemaiah?"

"People bring us only a little food—just a few very close friends. They do it in secret because they don't want to make trouble for themselves or me. But our little farm is doing well," he smiled. "Better than it ever has before. We have everything we need. God is good to us."

"Does your wife know about your visits here?" I asked him.

"No. I have never told her. If some of those spying priests should ask her about me, it would make things rather difficult. We here are the only ones who know. Someday I will tell her, but not yet."

"Does she know you're under censure by the church court?"

"Yes."

"What does she think about that?"

"She asked me one day if it was true—some of the women had told her. I told her there were some problems but that I could not discuss them with her yet. Then she asked if that was the reason that many people quit bringing food, and I told her it is. She's a good wife. Although she has said nothing more, I can tell that she really loves me, and I surely do love her. I don't know what I would do without her. She is a good mother, too. Once our children asked her why I don't help with the choir now, and she told them that I'm having some problems, but it will be all right because God will help us."

"I'd surely like to go and visit her," I said, "but—"

"No, no!" He shook his head. "We would all be in much trouble."

"If there is anything you feel I can do, be sure to

tell me."

"Just pray and teach us," Priest Shemaiah said. His brother-in-law nodded in agreement.

"This evening let's all kneel and each one pray before we begin," I suggested. "We have so much to talk to God about. He loves us and He's guiding us."

When we were seated once more, Shemaiah said, "Are you ready for more questions?"

Just then we heard a knock at the door. The startled look on my visitors' faces betrayed something of the tension they lived under. Martha answered the knock. Coming into the living room from the hallway, she said, "A nurse from the hospital wishes to speak with you."

Shemaiah clapped his hand over his mouth in relief, then whispered, "Please don't let her see us here."

Thankful for heavy draperies over the windows, I went into the hallway and shut the door behind me. Then I opened the front door and answered the nurse's questions. From then on we became more and more careful.

"Now for the questions," Shemaiah said. "Luke 14:25-27 and 33 is the problem."

"Will you read it for us?" I suggested.

" 'And there went great multitudes with him: and he turned, and said unto them, If any man come to me, and hate not his father, and mother, and wife, and children, and brethren, and sisters, yea, and his own life also, he cannot be my disciple. And whosoever doth not bear his cross, and come after me, cannot be my disciple.' 'So likewise, whosoever he be of you that forsaketh not all that he hath, he cannot be my disciple.' "

The priest looked up, shaking his head. "Does that *really* mean what it says? I read in 1 John 3:15—here it is, 'Whosoever hateth his brother is a murderer: and ye know that no murderer hath eternal life abiding in him.' And then there's Ephesians 5:28. I marked it, too. 'So ought men to love their wives as their own bodies. He that loveth his wife loveth himself.' Are there *two* kinds of people in God's kingdom—those who love and those who hate? Those who hate—they hate that they may follow Jesus? Maybe their reward is greater? What is a man supposed to do?"

I looked at Brother Adam and suggested that he answer.

"Well, let's turn to Matthew 10:37. Priest Peter, you may read this one," Brother Adam began.

" 'He that loveth father or mother more than me is not worthy of me: and he that loveth son or daughter more than me is not worthy of me.' "

"Jesus is saying that if we follow Him, we must make Him supreme in our lives," Adam explained. "He is not saying that we hate our families in the absolute sense, but only in a comparative sense. Consider, for example, a case where some members within a family will decide against Christ and persecute their own relatives who believe in Christ. What shall the Christian family members do? Yield to the others to make peace? No. They will follow Christ. At all cost they will remain loyal to Jesus. But even then, they will *love* their brother, their wife, their children, for that is the way of Christ."

"What about forsaking all for Christ?" Shemaiah continued, appearing more relieved.

"When we accept Jesus as the center of our life, we make Him supreme. All that we are and have are His even *before* we acknowledge it. But when we come to Him, we let Him know that we recognize and submit to the fact that not only ourselves but all our possessions are His. Our love for Him is so deep, our gratitude so great, that we say, 'Use me and everything I have in Your service.'

"God might ask us to leave our present place and move. He might request a large part of our money—or all of it—to be used in His service. Or He might summon us to some far-off land where we have nothing to really call our own. On the other hand, He might leave us right where we are, in our same house, with our family, our present job. The real question is *Who* or what *is supreme* in my life?"

"Then the monks who do not get married? What about them?" Priest Peter inquired. "Will their reward be greater? Will they be holier?"

"After God made Adam, what did He create next?" Brother Adam questioned.

"A wife for Adam," Priest Peter replied.

"When Isaac needed a wife, what did God do for him?"

"Helped Isaac's servant find one for him," Shemaiah answered, smiling.

"And what about Ruth and Boaz? Even the apostle Peter, who the Bible says left all and followed Jesus—we find him along with others of the apostles and Jesus at Peter's house. His wife's mother is sick. Jesus heals her. And she gets up and serves the group. There's not a hint that when Peter 'left all' that he dissolved all family ties. Jesus visits his home on a Sabbath afternoon and they remain into the evening taking care of sick people—physical bodies, no less. Jesus wanted people to be well and happy, to have happy, loving homes.

"When He looked for an illustration of how He loves the church, He called it His bride and He went on to use the love in a happy marriage to show His love for those who have chosen to accept His call to follow Him. Nothing in the Bible tells us that two people should not get married if they love God and recognize that their relationship will be for their good and the glory of God.

"When Paul wrote to Timothy he said that some would come with doctrines of devils and would forbid people to marry (1 Timothy 4:1, 3). But God does not prohibit us from marrying or having children. It was His purpose that we should have them.

"What was the first miracle that Jesus ever performed?"

"Jesus turned water into wine," Priest Peter answered.

"What was the occasion?"

"It was at a wedding feast," Priest Shemaiah said.

"Suppose Jesus had said, 'My friends, I can't make any wine for your feast. Don't you know marriage is wrong? You would be much holier if you never got married'? But He did no such thing. The wine He made was the best at the feast. There's no record that He even gave a discourse to His disciples at a later time about not getting married.

"When Paul wrote to Timothy about the qualifications for a bishop, he didn't say, 'Find a man who has never been married.' No, he said he should be 'the husband of one wife'—not two or three, but one. And of course he would not commit adultery."

LEARN OF ME

The priests sat for a while, just thinking.

At last Priest Shemaiah looked up. "Then what does it mean over here in James—?" He turned the pages of his Bible. "James 4:10—'Humble yourselves in the sight of the Lord, and he shall lift you up.'"

"Let's go back to verse 6," Brother Adam suggested. "James has described people who live according to the lusts of the flesh. But it says here that God resists—He opposes—the proud, 'but giveth grace unto the humble.' It continues, 'Submit yourselves therefore to God. Resist the devil, and he will flee from you.' Humility leads to submission to God's will. To those who yield, God gives grace. It was His grace that led them to their submission in the first place. And He continues to provide power to resist Satan. 'Draw nigh to God, and he will draw nigh to you,' James declares. He was near to us in the first place, but when we decide to accept Him, He moves in even closer, has a more intimate relationship with us. Then He asks us to cleanse our hearts and hands. How do we do this? We repent. Turning our lives around, we focus our spiritual gaze on Jesus as we mourn for our sins. Now James tells us, 'Humble yourselves in the sight of the Lord, and he shall lift you up.'

"We humble ourselves through repentance and confession. Each of us must recognize, admit, repent, and confess that he or she has lived after the flesh—that is, in opposition to God. Asking God to change us from a worldly person to a spiritual person,

79

we crucify the flesh. We are down in the pit of sin and we recognize it and long for deliverance. The Bible promises that God will lift us up. He does this by forgiving us and, cleansing us, giving us His own righteousness. No longer does He count us among sinners, but with His saints."

"It looks to me as though we would need to continue a life of humility," Priest Peter observed. "Otherwise we would soon be back living a fleshly life."

"Yes, this is why we carry our cross as we follow Jesus," Brother Adam explained. "We crucify the natural man all along the way, by repentance and confession."

"How can we keep on doing this—out in the world with so much going on?" Shemaiah questioned.

"Let's turn to Matthew 11:28-30," I suggested. "Brother Adam, would you?"

" 'Come unto me, all ye that labour and are heavy laden, and I will give you rest. Take my yoke upon you, and learn of me; for I am meek and lowly in heart: and ye shall find rest unto your souls. For my yoke is easy, and my burden is light.' "

"The burden everyone carries, as he or she walks in the flesh, is that of sin and its results," I commented.

"Jesus invites us to come to Him for rest. He pleads for us to take His yoke, to walk with Him. The yoke provides a means for His lifting our load and for putting us into step with Him. It brings us into harmony with His will and keeps us there. At any point we may lay off His yoke and go the way of the flesh. But the call is to take His yoke—to agree that the way of the flesh is not what we need, and to accept the way of the Spirit. Immediately this leads us to do the next thing—'learn of me' [Jesus]. To do so changes us, transforms our thoughts, our actions, our very lives. The lessons He teaches will be of Himself—*His* meekness and lowliness, *His* humility. As we learn them we will live the life of humility. It will be a life of recognition that God is our Creator, our Sustainer, our Saviour and Lord, and will lead to faith and obedience.

"And then Jesus says, 'Ye shall find rest unto your souls.' That is the reward of walking with Jesus. *Rest.* Our hearts will have a peace and trust that the fleshly, worldly, self-loving person never knows.

"Jesus adds, 'My yoke is easy, and my burden is light.' He does not claim there is no burden—but He does say that it is *light*."

BRIGHT LIGHT

A few nights later the two men returned with Priest Shemaiah began. "There's no time for visiting." After inquiring about Priest Peter's wife, we once more asked God for guidance and thanked Him that the priest's wife was well again. Then we opened our Bibles.

"What's the next question?" I asked. "We've not finished your list, have we?"

"Oh, no!" both men groaned.

"So?"

Priest Shemaiah's face clouded as he said, "I've been thinking about those saints. Yes, I can accept the idea that we shouldn't venerate them. The Lord *does* forgive. Jesus *is* our high priest, our advocate. God's people—all of them—are called *saints*. But—" Tears filled his eyes as he paused.

I waited.

He swallowed hard. "But—but—*Mary*. Saint Mary. Oh, I do love her! I can let the others go. But *Mary*. She is the mother of Jesus. I love Him. Can't I love *her*?" His voice was pleading.

"I love Mary too," I answered softly.

"You do? Does the Bible let you love *her*?" Now his voice held a tinge of hope.

"The Bible speaks of loving all people," I replied. "I think when we reach heaven, Mary will be one of the first people I will want to talk to. She must have been a kindly, loving, gentle person. Surely she loved God with all her heart. Because she was close to Jesus as He grew up, she could tell me many things about Him that others never could. I think she will care about all those who are saved—she'll care in a special way because she will really see that it is Jesus who saved them all. Yes, I would be so happy to see her!"

The priests leaned back and relaxed. "Then we don't have to forget her," Shemaiah remarked. "But doesn't she have *anything* to do with our salvation?"

"Do you remember the story in the Gospel of Luke that tells how Mary went to Elisabeth's home to visit?" I asked. "Let's turn to Luke 1:46, 47. Would you like to read it, Priest Peter?"

The priest read slowly: " 'And Mary said, My soul doth magnify the Lord, and my spirit hath rejoiced in God my Saviour.' "

"In whom did Mary rejoice?" I asked.

"In God, her Saviour," Shemaiah replied.

"Did Mary need a Saviour?"

"She must have, for she is rejoicing in God, her Saviour. God would not have been her Saviour if she hadn't needed one." He seemed thoughtful.

"Would we dare to assume that she was a sinner in need of a Saviour?" I questioned.

"It looks that way," Priest Peter responded.

"Jesus died for the sins of His mother, Mary, too? He was *her* Saviour?" A note of concern filled Shemaiah's voice.

"Have you found any place in the Bible that tells us that Mary was sinless or that she did not need a Saviour?" I questioned. The men shook their heads. "Is there any place that says we should pray to her?"

Again they shook their heads.

"Does Scripture say that she intercedes for us?"

"No," they agreed, "not that we have found. And we can't find anything to indicate that we should bow down to her picture or sing to her or venerate her," Shemaiah added. "But what *do* we do with her?" he pleaded.

"We love her. We respect her as one who had a real part—a part designed by God Himself—in being the mother of the One who came as our Saviour. Hers was an important work. But she well knew that she herself needed a Saviour. She never spoke of her role as being that of a Saviour or even an intercessor for others. But we can love her as the noble, courageous woman who responded to the summons by God to do a work to which no other woman has ever been called—or will be called—to do."

Priest Shemaiah nodded. "I'm glad I don't have to

tell her Goodbye forever in order to believe the Bible," he said, and we all agreed. "Now another question. Those men will come to ask me many things. I must be ready for them. What can we say about the Bible and tradition?"

"That's for you, Brother Adam," I smiled.

"Will you read to us 2 Timothy 3:16, 17, Priest Shemaiah?" he suggested.

" 'All scripture is given by inspiration of God, and is profitable for doctrine, for reproof, for correction, for instruction in righteousness: that the man of God may be perfect, throughly furnished unto all good works.' "

"How much of Scripture is inspired—God-breathed?" Brother Adam asked.

"All of it."

"What is it good for?"

"Doctrine, reproof, correction, instruction in righteousness that God's people may be perfect," he replied.

"Jesus showed that all doctrines taught in the church are not necessarily His doctrine," Adam continued. "In Matthew 15:9—let's look at it—Jesus says, 'In vain they do worship me, teaching for doctrines the commandments of men.' In verse 3, He asks, 'Why do ye also transgress the commandment of God by your tradition?' Mark 7:8 records some of His comments this way: 'For laying aside the commandment of God, ye hold the tradition of men.' Then again in Matthew 15:6 He declares, 'Thus have ye made the commandment of God of none effect by your tradition.'

"As we look at these passages we see two ways to go—according to God's commandments, which teach us truly how to worship Him, or according to man's tradition. But Jesus always says God's commandments are the guide. It is empty, *vain* worship to follow human tradition rather than God's commands."

Then Adam smiled and said, "Priest Peter, would you read Colossians 2:8 for us?"

" 'Beware lest any man spoil you through philosophy and vain deceit, after the tradition of men, after the rudiments of the world. and not after Christ,' " he read.

"Here again Scripture constrasts human tradition and Christ," Brother Adam commented, "but there is also a good tradition. Paul speaks of it in 2 Thessalonians 2:15—'Hold the traditions which ye have been taught, whether by word, or our epistle,' he says. But if we read the verses before this we find that the apostle is referring to the tradition of God's gospel. Paul never teaches us that we are to regard man's ideas as above God's Word."

Shemaiah sat with his head in his hands as his brother-in-law glanced his way a little uneasily. Then he stood up and walked around the room. Priest Peter looked at him—waiting, wondering.

"Uh, uh, those books wrapped in those expensive silk cloths—those are tradition," Shemaiah said as he straightened his blanket around his shoulders. "This Bible here in my hand that I carry around—it is God's Word. It's first. It's best. I check tradition by this Book." A pleased smile covered his face as his eyes sparkled in the firelight. "I'm glad it's that way." Then he sat down once more.

"Look at Psalm 119:105," I suggested.

He turned to the passage and read: " 'Thy word is

a lamp unto my feet, and a light unto my path.' " He nodded. "That's what it is—a light on a dark night."

"Now the mass," he continued. "Is that God's command or is it tradition? I can't find any place in the Bible that says we should do this. Here I am in the Most Holy Place with a cup of wine in my hand. I say a few words and I've turned wine into the blood of Christ! A few more words over the bread, and I've created God! Me! A sinful man who needs a Saviour—and God has given me the task of making the blood and flesh of God! It was God who created man. How can man, a created being, create God?"

"He can't!" Priest Peter exclaimed. "There's no way! Besides, the idea of offering—sacrificing Christ again and again! It makes no sense to me! Does the Bible say *anything*?"

"Let's look at Hebrews 9:28," Adam suggested.

Shemaiah found it: " 'So Christ was once offered to bear the sins of many.' 'Once offered'—'once offered.' He was offered once!" the priest exclaimed.

"Look over at verses 25 and 26," I suggested.

" 'Nor yet that he should offer himself often, as the high priest entereth into the holy place every year with blood of others; for then must he often have suffered since the foundation of the world: but now once in the end of the world hath he appeared to put away sin by the sacrifice of himself.' " Priest Shemaiah stared at me a moment.

"So we're not sacrificing Him again and again! We *aren't* creating. We *aren't* sacrificing! That's tradition. But the Bible—not tradition, but the *Bible*—says that Jesus broke bread and said, 'Take, eat: this is my body' and 'This cup is the new testament in my blood.' Now what does *this* mean?"

"Let's turn to 1 Corinthians 11:26, which is in the same passage you've mentioned," I said. "It reads 'For as often as ye eat this bread, and drink this cup, ye do shew the Lord's death till he come.' These are symbols reminding us of Jesus' death. We will have them until He comes again. Verse 25 says we drink the cup in remembrance of Him. Accounts of the Last Supper appear in Matthew 26:26-29, Mark 14:22-24, and Luke 22:19, 20. In each passage Jesus tells us to observe it 'in *remembrance* of me.' There is no reason to sacrifice Him again and again. He died once and only once."

"But why," Priest Peter protested, "does it say 'This is my body'? 'This is my blood which was shed'? It makes it sound as if it's really His body and blood."

"Yes, it does," I agreed. "But do you remember how Jesus said in other places, 'I am the vine,' 'I am the door,' 'I am the bread of life,' 'I am the water of life'—what did He mean?"

"Those were symbols," Shemaiah replied. "He was trying to tell us many things about Himself."

"That's right," Brother Adam agreed. "When He said He was the door, He was saying we could reach heaven only through Him—He was the only way out of sin into eternal life. And when He speaks of bread and wine He is employing symbols that remind us of His sacrifice for us. We accept this one sacrifice by faith and look forward with rejoicing to eating and drinking with Him in His heavenly kingdom. This also shows that we accept Him into our lives. He is as necessary for our spiritual life as food and drink are for our physical life."

"I've been thinking a lot about this lately," Shemaiah commented. He stood up again and walked around, pausing to stir the embers in the fireplace. "I can never participate in the mass again. I can't. I *can't!* I don't know what the church leaders are going to do with me. It could mean my life." Pausing in his restless pacing, he stared at the wall. "I love those people. The priests—I've grown up with them. We've had many wonderful hours together. They will hate me. I know they will."

Priest Peter nodded as he glanced my way.

Then Shemaiah sat down. "Let's pray," he whispered. "Each of us must pray. I want to follow God, not man's tradition. But I need courage. They are watching me more and more. Oh, I do love them— why, why don't *they* read their Bibles and choose to follow Jesus! His way is so much easier. He is my shepherd. I will listen to Him and follow Him by His grace. Let's pray."

BRIEF VISIT

"I love the Bible! Oh, I do love it!" Priest Shemaiah exclaimed when he came again. "It is like a bright light on a dark night. Some of my friends from down in the desert country told me the other day that the churches in that region are in serious trouble. They say the priests are tired of living there—it's hot and dusty. There is often hunger because of drought. So the priests have all moved away. Poor people! They have no one to confess to. No one to read the liturgy in the ancient, sacred language. They feel that there is no way for them to be saved unless they move near a priest. Otherwise, they fear they will burn forever in hellfire.

"But I assured them that all they really need to do is to get a Bible in their own language and read it. They will need to ask God to help them understand it, and they will need to decide to follow Him—to obey Him. Then He will teach them. And because they can confess their sins to Him, they don't need a priest for confessions." He smiled to himself. "I'm glad that God has taught me this. I like to tell it to others. Many are so relieved when they hear it that it makes me very happy.

"About hell—does God *really* burn sinners forever? Didn't we read in Romans 6:23 that the wages of sin is *death*? How can sinners burn forever if they are supposed to die?"

"Let's read Malachi 4:1," I suggested.

Shemaiah found it and began reading slowly: " 'For, behold, the day cometh, that shall burn as an oven; and all the proud, yea, and all that do wickedly, shall be stubble: and the day that cometh shall burn them up, saith the Lord of hosts, that it shall leave them neither root nor branch.'

"Well," he exclaimed, "that doesn't say they burn forever! They are *burned up!* More tradition! How many thousands of people I've told that the wicked will burn forever! Now I see that the ones who live forever are the ones who have accepted Jesus as their Saviour. His gift is eternal life, something the wicked don't have. The Bible makes it so easy!" Then his face sobered.

"I was called to our church court yesterday

morning. The priests and some governors were there, but my accusers didn't come. While we waited, they had a big discussion. They asked me many questions. I had my Bible, and I read the answers from it. You know how I put lines under the important texts. This has made it easy for me to teach people. I asked God to help me. My great High Priest, Jesus, was there. Because of this I was able to answer every question. At the end one of the most influential judges turned to the priests and said, 'A blind mule and a priest who does not teach truth are both useless. One and a half meters of cloth wrapped around a man's head is useless—it helps him only to get money. Why are our priests so ignorant? Why do you not read the Bible as Priest Shemaiah does? Why are you teaching lies when you could teach truth?' They argued with him so much that they forgot about me. My accusers never came, so we eventually went home.

"I have finally decided that I am going to leave the priesthood, but I will not make this known until after we return from giving out Bibles."

"How are things at home?" I asked. "Do you have food? Can you do any gardening?"

"Yes, we still have food, though almost no one gives us any now. People do not speak to us. The children at school are making it difficult for my children. But I have decided that I cannot teach tradition. I am so happy—I have such peace when I open the Word of God to them. It is a light in a dark night. God will care for us. I know He will.

"I think Priest Peter and I should be going. Since I am almost constantly being watched, I don't want them to put me in prison before I go to help with the Bibles."

MORE ENCOUNTERS

Two nights later Priest Shemaiah visited a patient in the hospital. Then quietly he stopped by to see me. The moon was full on that clear, cool night, and I was out looking at my garden. When I saw the priest approaching I called Pastor Adam to translate. He also would be helping to give Bibles to the pilgrims.

It seemed strange to be visiting outside where onlookers might see us talking together, but Priest Shemaiah seemed not to care. We laid our plans carefully. The three of us would leave together on the first flight in just two days. Others would follow later.

Then the man spoke seriously: "I have decided—really decided—to follow Jesus no matter what it costs. Several times I have been called to court. Many men have been there. They ask so many questions, but they do nothing because my accusers don't come. God will help me. I know He will. He has promised, and I can see that He is helping me every day."

Under the dark evergreen trees we talked for some time, then prayed and went our separate ways.

Two days later we went to the tiny airport, each from a different direction. We managed to board unnoticed by anyone except the pilot, who was a Christian friend, and a few children.

For the next several days we witnessed the marvelous work of God as we distributed hundreds of Bibles to priests and thousands of Gospels to the laypeople. God blessed Shemaiah in a wonderful way, and his faith grew stronger and stronger.

By the time we returned, a week later, everyone in our little town knew that he had gone to give out Bibles—and with heretics.

He was soon summoned to court, but the judge said, "It does not matter to us whether men worship the moon or idols—every person should have a right to choose who or what he worships. Why do you call this man again and again? Where are his accusers? They do not show up, but he comes as an obedient citizen."

The session closed with no verdict, and the priest went home.

That evening he told Adam and me about it. "You've cut your beard," Brother Adam commented.

"Yes," Shemaiah replied. Then he described the court session that morning. "Afterward I went home and cut my beard. In just a few days the church will have a great religious celebration here in town. Thousands of people will gather. No priest ever cuts his beard. But I've decided that this is the time to let them know I've changed. I want them to ask me *Why*. Then I can tell them how to come to Jesus as their Saviour. I feel very sorry to see so many people trying to work their way to heaven. They must learn that there is another way. I will wear my turban and priest's clothes, but they can tell in a minute that I am not in agreement with the teachings."

We prayed earnestly that evening. Such a move could mean his life.

A few days later he returned. "How is it going?" we asked.

"Very well," he replied. "Many people pass and shake their heads in disgust. They mutter 'Heretic.' Some even shout it. But others come to me in secret and ask *Why*. Then I tell them of God's Word. Some want Bibles. Do you have any that I can give them?"

I brought him several.

The whole town was astir. Priest Shemaiah, the one whom the high priest had reared—who was to succeed the high priest in that large, beautiful church on the hill—had turned *heretic*. But he had not planned to.

"I only want to follow Jesus," he would say again and again. "If only we could have all read our Bibles and followed Him together. I thought that they would want to. The way of Jesus is so much easier."

One evening he asked me for $10. "Usually I pay $10 per year for my land," he explained. "The payment is due in four months, but the court has told me I must bring the money now. I don't have $10 anywhere."

Quickly I gave him the money, and he left.

The next day he returned, and laughing, he explained, "I took the money to the court, but they gave it back. They were really embarrassed and admitted that it was a trap. The officials thought I didn't have $10, and they were sure I had no friends to give it to me. They planned to put me in prison if I didn't pay it. But here it is!"

"Keep it," I said, smiling. "You need it."

There seemed to be no end to the harassing. A few days later the court again summoned him. "You are not working for the church. We will take away your land," the officials declared.

With a sad heart he said quietly, "It is yours—part of it. You may take the part that belongs to the church."

"They are trying to make me give up my faith," he

said to us. "I wonder what God will do. Sometimes I'm afraid; sometimes I'm not. Let's pray again."

A few days later the authorities called him in and told him that he would have to pay a high rent on the land he farmed.

The forty days had gone by. Soon the two months would be past. Then the patriarch would arrive to question him. Joy and sadness mingled in his heart.

In the meantime there was a Bible convention scheduled to meet in a faraway city. "Would you like to go?" I asked the priest. "I will pay your way."

"Yes!" he exclaimed.

After arranging with his brother-in-law Peter to care for his family, he left in secret to spend several weeks. I had work to do in another far-off city. The church councils would have time to wait and wonder. They seemed unable to believe that a priest could abandon the church tradition.

Sometimes I wondered how our friend could bear it, but he loved his Saviour, and he cared deeply for those who opposed him. Surely God was giving him grace and strength.

Several weeks later he returned home, and I arrived soon after.

That evening the judge came to see me. "I have many questions," he said. "I've been reading my Bible. May I come to learn from you?"

"Yes, we'll be glad to have you."

"It must be in secret."

We set a time.

"I will help arrange for groups of people to receive Bibles," he whispered as he left.

Soon after, Priest Shemaiah arrived, his face radiant. "The Bible convention—it was *wonderful!*"

94

he exclaimed. "I learned many things. Oh, I do love God! I want to tell others of what I have learned! May I come and study each day? Will you and Brother Adam help me?" He looked pleadingly at me.

"Yes, I believe we can do that."

So each day he came. He poured out his heart to God and asked for strength to bear each trial. And in those sober days we saw what God does for those who put their trust in Him.

NEVER AGAIN

"I'm in a tangle every day with the leaders," Priest Shemaiah commented a few days later. "They ask, 'Why have you left us?' I tell them I haven't left them. Oh, sister, I love them! I love them! I've grown up with them. I can't leave them. They told me this week that I can't come to church anymore. That hurts. I love them, and I love to worship God with them.

"One saw me with my Bible and said, 'I don't ever want to see your unclean Book.'

"Yesterday some men came from several days walk away. Having heard that I had gone crazy, they journeyed all this way to see a crazy priest. They asked me many questions to determine whether I had lost my mind.

"My wife asked me if I really believe the Bible above tradition. I told her that I do. She thinks I'm teasing everybody.

"But I'll tell you when I hurt the worst. You know I've been going to the church where you attend. But nobody will look at me or say "Good morning" except you and four or five others. The rest all turn their backs to me." Tears filled his eyes. "Where can I go to have Christian friends?"

I knew he spoke the truth. "These people are afraid of you," I explained. "They think that you are a spy and find it difficult to believe that you have changed so much."

He nodded.

"It's like the time that Saul the persecutor became a Christian. The people were afraid, but if you continue to be faithful, they will learn to trust you."

"I understand," he replied patiently. "I will wait and trust God."

A few days later he informed me, "The church leaders are trying another way to get me back with them. They have offered to give me more responsible work with bigger pay and more land, but I have told them I cannot do this unless they allow me to teach according to the Bible. I'll still go to church—I love the people, and I love God. But I cannot participate as a priest."

Saturday night he was back. "One of those two officials arrived for the big council about me," he announced. "The priests' charges were that I had quit working as a priest without consulting them and that I still attend church. Really, I didn't quit. I'd be there yet if they would allow me to teach the Bible. Well, anyway, they asked the patriarch, 'What shall we do?'

"The patriarch said, 'Nothing. He has a right to search for truth. You cannot forbid him to search.'

"They became extremely angry and demanded,

'Are you a heretic too? We will not allow him to bury any of his family in our cemetery, and he cannot be buried there.'

"The patriarch told them, 'That's all right. I'd rather be buried out in the pasture.'

"They didn't say more about me after that. Later he left."

The next day—Sunday—he returned with Pastor Adam. He had gone to church at seven in the morning. Now about noon he stood in my doorway with a look of pain, as if he had had a physical beating. "I'm glad you didn't attend church this morning," he said with a deep sigh, unable to keep the tears back. "It was terrible, terrible!" He shook his head as though he couldn't believe the truth of his words. "There was much, much trouble. They told me never to set foot inside that church again—not even to walk in the churchyard. They were shouting and screaming at the top of their voices. They told me they would kill me if I came near the church. I love them! Oh, I love them! Why can't I worship God with them?" he cried. "Never, never again to go into that church—just because I'm reading my Bible and searching for truth. They told the judge that he is not allowed there either." He paused and wept aloud, then added, "One more thing they said—they told me to tell you"—his voice was gentle, full of grief—"they told me to tell you *never* to come there again or they will kill you."

"Me?" I asked in surprise. "What have *I* done? I gave them Bibles and they were so happy. I've helped their sick. Many of the priests have been my patients. I've loved to worship with them in their church. And they've told *me* not to come?" My own tears flowed down my cheeks as I thought of those early-morning excursions through the dewy grass, of climbing the stone pathway while birds caroled their praises to God and priests chanted psalms. I reflected on the many beautiful sunrises and the kindly people I had met there. Now it was all over. All over because I had carried to them a bright light on a dark night. The priest and I sat in dumb silence while tears drenched our faces.

Several days later another job assignment took me away for a few weeks. But I was thankful that Pastor Adam was willing to study with Brother Shemaiah while I was away. The former priest had a long list of questions—Where are the dead now? Where is heaven? Will we know Jesus when He comes? What is the judgment? What is the resurrection going to be like? How can we understand the book of Revelation? Who should pay tithe? What are the beasts in the book of Daniel? What is the millennium? Should we fast forty days in Lent? He soon had pages of notes in his notebook.

"I'm so happy, so happy!" he would exclaim at the end of each study. "I'm so sad, yet so happy. The Bible is the brightest light in the darkest night I've ever lived. I wish all my friends wanted to study. But I *am* reading with many other priests. They come to me in secret, one at a time, and we learn together."

I longed to tell him that several of them had been studying with me, individually and in secret. And I was glad that Adam had time to translate and that Martha would be there to encourage them.

CURSED

During my absence I felt great concern about my friends so far away. The night before I left, Brother Shemaiah had talked a long while with me. "I've been cursed by the priests," he said. "The people everywhere look at me with the 'evil eye.' They began this on the Sunday when they sent me from the church. I didn't know it that morning, but when I went home in the afternoon after seeing you, I found my wife crying pitifully. She explained that the priests had come to our house and told her that they had cursed me and I would soon die." He sighed, then continued.

"I told her that what they said was not true—I would not die. Someday I will, but not now. God will not let those priests have any reason to think that they can kill a man who reads his Bible—not by cursing him, anyway. This is not the right time for it to happen. I'm sure it isn't! God is going to fool them. I know He will!" He laughed in amusement at how God would outwit those who cursed him. Then he said softly, "I must be going now. But let's pray first."

We had much to pray about these days. Often while I was gone I wondered what would happen to these spiritual fledglings who were just learning to fly.

Two weeks later I arrived back home. In the afternoon the priest brought his entire family to see me. We talked of Jesus and of heaven. Deborah, his wife, asked many questions, and we searched the Bible for a long while to discover answers. She was overjoyed that the entire family was well and happy.

That evening Shemaiah returned with Brother Thomas. He seemed deeply worried. "No one—not a person—visits our house," he said. "Even the girl that carried water from the public supply stays away. No one brings us any food." Tears welled up in his eyes.

"The other day my wife's parents came to take my wife and children home with them. They said, 'Your husband is cursed. He has left the true faith to join the heretics. You and your children must leave with us. We will take you while he is gone from the house.' They were extremely angry."

"What did your wife say?" I asked, remembering that she had come with him to see me only a few hours before.

"She told them, 'I have lived with him for fourteen years while he was not in trouble. Why should I leave him now while he is in deep trouble? He needs me now more than he has ever needed me before. I do not understand why he thinks as he does, but he needs me. We were married in the church—married until one of us dies. I cannot go.'

"Her parents cursed our whole family, then left," he said with sadness.

MY CROSS

Daily we searched God's Word with much prayer.

One day I asked, "Where is Priest Peter? He has not visited for a long while."

Shemaiah nodded his head. "He studies with me in secret. I tell him what I've learned here, but he's afraid to come. My brother-in-law doesn't want to be excommunicated."

About ten days passed. It had been exactly one month since that terrible Sunday morning when the church leaders had banished Shemaiah. Early in the morning someone knocked on my door. Opening it, I found him. "My wife is very sick," he said. "Can you go and see her?"

After finding a translator, we made our way to the house. There she lay almost motionless. Weakly she pointed to a huge abscess on her chest. Indeed, she was an extremely ill woman.

"Our baby is sick too," the priest said with an anxious face.

I checked her over and commented, "Probably pneumonia. We need to take both of them to the hospital. Can you care for your other three children?" How I wished the members of his newfound church would make friends with his family, but they were still afraid of him.

We put his wife and child to bed in the hospital, and the doctor wrote the orders. "They are both very sick," he said seriously. "I hope they live, but they might not. We will ask God to heal them according to His will."

"It's the curse," Brother Shemaiah worried. "My wife has not yet decided to really follow Jesus. She's loyal to me, but she's not sure about following Him. Satan is trying to destroy her. We must pray."

And pray we did. The whole town was watching—waiting. Would this cursed woman live or die? No kind friend entered her home to care for her children.

"It's my cross," Shemaiah observed quietly. "I have taken it up to follow Jesus. I don't think God will let her die—nor our dear baby. But I have heard the Shepherd's voice. I will follow, whatever happens."

Martha and I cooked food and took it to him and his children, and Martha carried water from the public supply for them. The people would not allow Shemaiah or his children near the water source.

Often, as I was caring for the mother and child, I prayed that God would spare them if it was His will. I was thankful that another nurse would work extra for me so I had more time for this family.

A few days later the happy mother walked home, carrying her infant in her arms as onlookers shook their heads—some in disgust and some in wonder.

That evening Shemaiah came to study. We had a praise service; then I asked, "Do you have food to eat?"

"God has been very good to us."

I pressed him: "What has He done to feed you?"

"He has done much," he replied, evading the question.

"What did your family have to eat yesterday besides the cooked food I sent?"

"We ate roasted barley seed."

"Did you have anything else?"

"No."

"What did you eat today?"

"Roasted barley seed."

"Nothing else?"

"No."

"You have nothing in your garden?"

"The drought has killed it all."

"Roasted barley seed. You mean you are using the barley you plan to plant when the rains come?"

He nodded.

"Your potatoes are finished?"

"Yes, long ago."

"How long have you been eating only roasted barley seed?" I asked as I thought of the many pounds of potatoes he had brought months before.

"About two weeks," he said.

"Why didn't you say something? I am so sorry," I said. "You always seemed so cheerful, and you didn't hint that things were this bad."

"God has been so good to us. I don't ever want Him to hear me complain," he answered.

Giving him some food from my cupboard, I told him I would visit them the next morning. He poured out his gratitude to God and to me, picked up the box, and went home.

Then I hurried to the doctor's wife to tell her of the problem. She gave me a large box of powdered milk and money enough to feed the family for several weeks.

Shemaiah's wife stood in the doorway the next morning when I arrived at their house with the gifts. Tears of joy flowed down her cheeks when I put the money in her hands. "Praise God! Praise God!" she exclaimed again and again.

That evening her husband and Pastor Adam came to study. "Do you remember those verses we read in Matthew months ago, where it says the birds don't plow, but God feeds them?" asked Brother Shemaiah with a big smile.

"Yes."

"Well, I can't plow—there's no use since there's

no rain. Besides, the ox I used belongs to both my neighbor and me. Since I was excommunicated, the only days that he will allow me to have the ox is Saturday or Sunday. He knows I'll not plow then, for I keep both Sabbaths. And he won't plow those days either. So I've had to let God care for me as He does the birds. I've been trying Him out. This is why I didn't tell you my problems—I was telling them to Him. I waited and waited. When my children would say, 'Are you sure God will help us?' I always told them He would. But last night my faith was almost ready to break. We had enough seed for only one more day.''

STILL SEARCHING

"I want to know about the two Sabbaths. Why do you have only one?'' Brother Shemaiah asked one evening.

"What I want you to tell me is why you have two?'' I replied.

"I don't know.'' He shook his head. "Genesis 2:1-3 talks about *the* Sabbath, *the* seventh day. Exodus 20:8-11 says that *the* seventh day is *the* Sabbath. It talks about six days to work and the *seventh* being *the* Sabbath, not the sixth and seventh, or seventh and first. The Gospels are even more specific. Look at Luke 23:56 and 24:1: 'rested *the* sabbath day according to the commandment.' And then the *real* problem: *the first day* of the week! Luke 23:54 states that the day before the sabbath was the preparation day. So it's 'preparation day,' 'Sabbath,' 'first day.' '' He shook his head in bewilderment. "It looks to me as if God meant for me to plow on Sunday! I could have my mule one day, anyway. But let's study some more.''

We did. His questions came fast: Didn't Jesus change the day when He was resurrected? Does it make any difference what day we keep? Hasn't the calendar been altered or time lost? Who did transfer the day? How did we get two Sabbaths? and on and on. For days we pored over Scripture.

Finally he announced one evening, "I've decided to keep the seventh-day Sabbath. But I've also decided not to plow on Sunday. Nothing could make the priests and others angrier than for me to do that. I think it would be wrong for me to antagonize them over something that can be avoided. Someday I'll have my own ox and I can plow when I wish. There's no water now anyway. But you will pray that I'll get a mule, won't you?''

He thought a moment. "No water. That brings up another question. When the Bible speaks of baptism there's a river around—not just a pitcher. Jesus and the eunuch both went into the water, and Paul speaks of being buried in baptism. The priest sprinkled me when I was born, but oh, I want to be baptized! I want to go down into the water with Jesus. I want to join your church. Can't you tell me more?''

We sat by the crackling fire and talked about this symbol of dying to the world and walking in newness of life.

"What about your wife?" Pastor Adam asked. "Does she want to be baptized?''

"No. Deborah has not learned enough yet about following Jesus. She has not really left our traditions, though she is not allowed to attend our church. But we are studying, and she comes here to learn sometimes. Next Sabbath she plans to visit church.

"But can't I be baptized even if she isn't? Deborah recognizes me as the leader in our home. She will not be angry, and will follow later."

"Brother Shemaiah," Adam, the church pastor, replied, "we will be happy to baptize you when you really understand the principles that our church adheres to. You have heard the call of Jesus and have chosen to follow Him. Let's study a few more things so that when you are baptized you won't have to say, 'Oh, I didn't know the church understands the Bible to say that.' We want you to be comfortable with our beliefs. Besides, you know the drought we're having. There's no water in the river, and we don't have enough to fill the baptistry! So let's go ahead and study and continue asking God for rain."

Brother Shemaiah nodded with a smile, then said seriously, "We need to help the church members not to be afraid of me."

I felt a twinge of pain when I recalled that after all these weeks he still went out behind the church and stood alone during the intermission between the Sabbath school class period and the worship service. After church three or four of us would shake hands with him. He would hold his head high as he grasped the hands of his two children and hurried out the gate after several vain attempts to speak to some of the members.

Yes, we needed to pray for water and for the church.

PARTING GIFT

The days went by too fast. In one week I would depart for my homeland, probably never to return.

"Come to our house," Brother Shemaiah said. "Bring your camera and take our picture. We want you always to remember us."

"I'll be happy to," I exclaimed. "But be sure I'll never forget you even if I have no picture on paper."

He smiled. "I know—but we want you to come."

Friday afternoon I went. Sunday I would be leaving. It seemed too much to think about. Although I had never been back to the church on the hill, I still had a warm place in my heart for the people. Walking along the dusty road, I saw some here and there that I knew. At last I came to the humble little home where Shemaiah's family waited for me.

It was hard to focus the camera as I blinked away the tears. How does a photographer get people to smile when she's wiping away tears and they're crying in their hearts? But they smiled anyway, and I've been glad ever since when I've looked at those photos.

The pictures finished and the visiting ended, we all stood there, reluctant to part. We prayed. Then I turned to go.

"Wait," Brother Shemaiah said. "I want to give you a gift." He reached out and handed me his brass cross—the cross he had carried all his years as a priest, the one that people had kissed ten thousand times and more—the one that he had fingered nervously so many times as we had studied.

"Thank you, Brother Shemaiah, but how can I take *this* from you? You might want it as a reminder of days gone by."

"No, I want you to have it. I have planned this for many months—ever since you explained what it means to take up my cross. I have taken up my cross and followed Jesus. Now I don't need this anymore. You take it. It's the most precious object I ever owned, other than my little parchment Gospel of John. You gave me this Bible, this bright light that shines on a dark night." As he spoke he looked down at the Bible under his arm. He carried it everywhere he went.

How could I express my deep gratitude for such a gift? I accepted it with feelings of joy that none can understand unless they have watched the miracle of conversion unfold before their own eyes.

Thanking him, I walked back alone along the dusty road. As I glanced out toward a meadow, a flood of memories came to mind. Eighteen months before, there had been a special holy day with dozens of priests in colorful garb singing and dancing as they traveled across the pasture in joyful procession. Priest Shemaiah had led it, his face aglow.

Just now I paused to recapture the scene.

I had been standing there watching, along with thousands more. As the procession moved toward where I waited, it seemed I heard a voice: Sophia, that priest in the lead. Pray for him. Go to his church and pray—pray for him. Someday he will become a Seventh-day Adventist Christian.

Now here I was, holding the very cross that he had carried in the procession.

POSTLUDE

Eleven years ago next month the Potato Man brought the first basket of potatoes to Teresa and me. Less than a year later we said Goodbye. Shortly afterward the rains came, and he was baptized in the nearby river. The officials imprisoned him several times. Twice he was beaten. The authorities seized most of his land. There seemed no letup from trouble.

Suddenly there was a revolution, and a new power took control. The new government forbade religious persecution and freed Brother Shemaiah, returning some of his land to him. God blessed his efforts at farming his few acres so that he and his family were able to subsist, though they frequently were in deep trials.

Faithfully Brother Shemaiah studied his Bible with others. His wife and four of his children have been baptized. Six years ago his new church appointed him to do evangelism. His warm letters tell of many baptisms of people he has studied with.

The brass cross lies in my trunk, where I keep some of the other precious gifts that loving people have given me, reminding me that "God so loved the world, that he gave his only begotten Son, that whosoever believeth in him should not perish, but have everlasting life" (John 3:16).

To Curious Readers

Some problems arose as I wrote this story. The first involved the matter of Bible translations. The priest used one translation in his own language, the translator often employed a different version in that language, and I used the King James Version. Often I found myself explaining the meaning of the text as well as the Old English vocabulary of the King James Version. My translator, whose Bible version had been made primarily from the English King James Version, would compare Priest Shemaiah's Bible with his, since the priest's translation was a modern version of that land. Now, as I write this story in English for an audience of another language, I find that in order to make the points clear, I must explain the King James text in a manner that would be clear to Priest Shemaiah if he were an English-speaking person with an English Bible in his hand. Because of this, I do not claim that the dialogue is precise.

Nor do I claim that it always came in the exact order here given, for the reader must remember that I have condensed almost a year of studies and visits into one small book.

While I kept a diary during that period and recorded happenings and often what we were studying at a given time, I may not have always correctly attributed an idea or thought to the individual who actually said it.

At times Priest Shemaiah found pastors with whom he talked. Rather than make the book cumbersome with minute details of who and what, I have put what he learned from those conversations into our account of Bible studies since that material does not change the story, but helps the reader to understand Priest Shemaiah's thinking.

I would not wish to leave the impression that I—or Brother Adam—always had answers as readily as it would appear in this book, for we at times had to ask Priest Shemaiah to give us time to search for answers. Then we would discuss these later.

Nor did I myself always understand deeply what I was finding and passing on. Indeed, as the studies progressed I often wondered at the light on Priest Shemaiah's face and his deep joy—and his tremendous courage in each crisis. As the days passed I became painfully aware that I was missing a relationship with God that this man now possessed. When I returned to my homeland, I set about to study and to respond as never before to what I read. I began to realize that this positive response at each step was what made the difference. The texts we had read to him began to make a great deal more sense to me. It rolled in on me like a cloud that though I thought that I believed in salvation by faith in Jesus Christ, I too had not understood it. The word *forgiveness* became the sweetest word I had ever heard. To be forgiven by God Himself—where could greater joy be found! Then it was that I, too, grasped in a much deeper way what the words *cross, flesh,* and *world* meant. Because of this I have taken the liberty to use a few more texts and deepen the explanation, though we probably did not do this in a few places in the actual studies.—The Author.